SHAll We eat outside?

You have a go

YOU wash I'll dry

I'll have the same as you.

TASTY

Shall We add more!

let's just USE our hands!

YOU try some!

ISBN 978-1-9998727-0-0

2nd Revised Edition | Copyright Marlborough School © 2017

Feed

A cookbook from a Cornish school kitchen –
freshly prepared by a hungry young chef
and served up by plucky parents.

Jessica Oughton
Marlborough School Kitchen

Sponsored by Sames + Littlejohns and LanesHealth

"Feed shows just how much you can do in a tiny school kitchen - if you've got the support of brilliant teachers and parents.
It's packed with gorgeous recipes, and lovely ideas!"

Jamie Oliver

"Feed is a genuinely lovely and really practical cookbook. The recipes are just terrific - I really want to cook and eat them all, from the spicy keema beef to the nettle pizza, the cauliflower cheese soup to the golly gosh green sauce. Feed also spreads the vital knowledge that learning to cook delicious healthy food makes a massive difference to the well-being of children, families, schools and communities. And it shows something really important - that great school food should really just be a scaled up version of great home cooking. This book deserves to be a huge success, because it will definitely enrich the lives of everyone who uses it."

Hugh Fearnley-Whittingstall

Introduction

1. Hello, I'm Jess

4. In the back garden

6. Let's go foraging!

10. Kids in the kitchen

14. Kitchen equipment

Main dishes – the whole shebang!

20. Smoked mackerel kedegree

22. Ham, leek and pea soup

24. Cauliflower and kale macaroni cheese

26. Luscious lamb and coconut curry

28. Curried parsnip soup

30. Warming beef and butternut stew

32. Fancy pants smoked salmon pasta

34. Sweet beet halloumi burgers

36. Cauliflower cheese soup

38. Happy homity pies

40. Squash and goats cheese lasagne

42. Crispy breaded mackerel

44. Stack 'em up savoury pancakes

46. Pasta con le sarde

48. Cheesy leek pasties

50. Spicy keema beef

52. Store cupboard tomato and sesame soup

54. Turkey and courgette burgers

56. Monday night's chicken pie

58. Saffron squid stew

60. Nettle pizza

62. Chocolate bean chilli

64. Falafel scotch eggs

Everything in a jar

68. Humble hummus

69. Cucumber tzatziki

70. Quick pickled chillies

72. Razor sharp lemon curd

73. Really wild garlic pesto

74. Super-speedy guacamole

76. Honey mustard dressing

77. Golly gosh green sauce

78. Nutty red pesto

Punchy puddings

82. Blackberry yoghurt cake

84. Spiced milk pannacotta

86. Oranges and lemons flapjack

88. Five minute pomegranate and lemon curd bowl

90. Foraged flower power fritters

92. Sherbet blood orange plate

94. Tropical rice pudding

96. Brilliant banana-pops

98. Apple and elderberry crumble

Sides, drinks and other bits!

102. Smoked mackerel pâté stars

104. Crispy crunchy kale

105. Buttery beetroot

106. Celeriac and potato gratin

108. Root veg rosties

110. A most colourful coleslaw

112. Cheesy polenta triangles

114. Chorizo patatas bravas

116. Lazy sweet potato chips

118. Show stealing garden salad

120. Popeye's cheese straws

122. Fruity crisps

124. Overnight tray bake loaf

126. Grilled chewy flatbreads

128. Speedy soda bread

130. Squash smoothie

131. Banana shake

132. Party pink lemonade

134. Wobbly white sauce

135. Cheat's puff pastry

136. Big fat tomato sauce

Hello,
I'm Jess

My day job is to feed people, but not just any ordinary people... children.

Children are extraordinary. They have imaginations as big as planets, energy levels longer than AA batteries, inquisitive minds that leave even the brainiest adult puzzled. Above all they are like sponges: listening, observing and absorbing everything that surrounds them. They question with the 'ifs', the 'buts' and the 'maybes'.

But now, it was our turn to question and explore a pretty ambitious possibility. Here at Marlborough School we wanted to produce our own cookbook, to tell the world what we have been getting up to in our little kitchen here in Falmouth, Cornwall.

But where do you start? Rewind two years. I had been working with food in various guises for a while: waiting on tables in restaurants, cooking in cafés, baking in bakeries and at that time I was cheffing for families on their holidays. I was looking for a job with roots, something to throw all my energy at, when I saw the school was advertising for a creative and inspiring school chef.

At the time it looked to me as if things were changing with food in schools. The School Food Plan had just been published and the Government was committed to it, along with the introduction of Universal Infant Free School Meals in 2014. The job sounded like a real challenge, but it was the sort of avenue I was looking for. It was no coincidence that Marlborough was advertising at this point, research has shown links between good food, happiness and attainment and this wasn't rocket science to them, it was something they already knew. Now with the UIFSM funding in the pipeline, their hands were untied and the red tape was gone. They could start to implement changes. BIG CHANGES!

Along with big changes comes uncertainty, but, luckily for us, the parents at the school really embraced our vision for school lunches. They supported us, not just because they knew the importance of a good midday meal to a child's daily learning but also because they saw the bigger picture. To surround our pupils at lunchtimes with fresh, local, homemade food will promote a long term cultural respect and knowledge of the importance of eating well.

Long gone were chicken nuggets and yellow custard pudding and here came beetroot burgers and banana lollies!

We serve around 200 meals to hungry children every day. At home, thankfully, you don't have to. But the principles of learning how to prepare tasty, locally sourced, healthy food remain the same – whether your job is to feed 2 people or 200.

And so our idea came to life, how could we use what we have learnt in the school kitchen and put it into context at home... make a cookbook of course!

We knew we couldn't do it on our own, so we put word out and a couple of parents put up their hands to help. Luckily, one was a designer and photographer and the other a copywriter. We sat down, bounced loads of ideas around and before we knew it, our cookbook Feed was becoming a reality.

A plan was hatched and it went from there. We aimed to produce a cookbook that was a celebration of what we had achieved at Marlborough: a celebration of the things we grow, gather, buy, cook and eat.

For two years we have beavered away, photographing recipes and writing in between the day jobs. It hasn't been easy; there have been highs and lows. At points we wanted to put it on hold, we thought we were taking on more than we could chew, but we kept on going, knowing that we were creating something special.

Feed is a celebration of communal eating, enjoying fantastic natural flavours and having an open mind to new ideas. So roll up your sleeves, grab your apron, turn the oven on and let's start cooking! (Obviously remembering to wash your hands first!)

In the
back garden

The garden is a really important part of our school, not only do we have a weekly Gardening Club but it's our outdoor classroom that we all share.

The garden is a great place to immerse children in the natural environment and it's amazing what you can grow even when your time is short and your space is small.

Children love planting seeds, nurturing the plants while they grow and better still harvesting the produce and eating them! We think it's really important that children are given a basic understanding of how we grow food. Not only do they learn something as they grow but they are more likely to give foods or ingredients a try when they have grown them themselves.

A great and easy starting point is popping to your local garden centre and buying a selection of herbs. Save a few old baked beans cans, washed of course, you can get the children to decorate them (be careful of sharp edges). Place some good compost in the cans and plant up, give them a good water and then stick them on a doorstep, window sill or if you have a fence attach them to this. Not only will they look pretty but they are filled with edibles! Our upper school playground is adorned with beautifully decorated cans with a rainbow of colour from what grows within.

Where you have a place for a hanging basket you can get different varieties of trailing fruit and vegetables. I have grown tomatoes and strawberries this way and it's a great space saving solution.

If you have the space to put a raised bed in your garden it's well worth the effort. In my garden I have an old fishing box that I found on a beach; it's perfect as it's already got holes in the bottom for drainage. It doesn't even have to be a conventional container - think outside the box. Old tyres, bath tubs, wellyboots, toilets... anything that can contain earth and is able to have holes in it will be good.

Even if you have no garden but have always fancied having a veg patch put your name down for an allotment. You'll bring home seasonal fruit and veg by the bucket load... as long as the slugs don't get there first!

Let's go foraging!

Children love foraging – I've found that they are much more likely to experiment with new flavours and textures if they're outside.

The outdoors is so much more unpredictable and exciting than a kitchen table so it brings out a sense of exploration that's otherwise hidden.

I've also found that the more involved children get in aspects of food production, the more likely they are to eat it. Our school children are always proud to show off their haul after a foraging trip, and eager to see what becomes of it.

Blackberries have to be one of the most satisfying things to forage for with children because they're basically free sweets. When we actually manage to bring some back to school (rather than munching them as we pick), I often use them to make a blackberry yoghurt cake (see page 82).

Foraging for nettles is also great fun, and I'm always surprised at how keen children at Marlborough are to give it a go, despite the odd sting. I usually give them the option of wearing rubber gloves, and teach them how to pick leaves without touching their upper surface (the undersides of nettle leaves don't sting you at all).

Nettles are amazing: they're packed with magnesium, calcium and iron, and in my opinion are much more flavoursome than any shop bought greens. I love steamed nettles, seasoned, and with a knob of butter on top or nettle tops fried with chopped up bacon. Pick just the top 2–3 pairs of leaves – these are the freshest, and most tender. For a great, easy recipe with nettles, see our nettle pizza on page 60.

Wild garlic and three-cornered leek are other foraging favourites of mine – both are easy to identify – three-cornered leek (more like a juicy spring onion than a leek) has a stem that has three raised ridges running down its stem. Wild garlic has broad, flat leaves, with flowers that look like exploding fireworks. Both plants smell strongly of garlic or onion, and are relatively easy to identify (although always follow the foraging rules opposite). For a great, simple and delicious alternative to shop bought pesto, see my recipe on page 73 for a really wild garlic pesto.

We're lucky to have several large bushes of overgrown nasturtiums just outside the school gates. If you haven't tried these, you need to: peppery, like rocket, but with a juicy, fragrant added flavour, both the leaves and flowers are the perfect finishing touch to a simple salad. Some of the children at Marlborough take a real pride in arranging their own salads, like ours on page 118.

When foraging, it's always best to stick to some basic rules, especially with children. Here are mine:

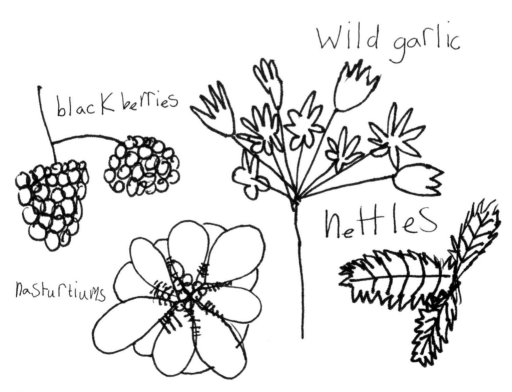

blackberries

Wild garlic

nettles

nasturtiums

Foraging rules

Identification

Never eat anything that you can't positively identify. This rule often puts people off foraging as they think that they need to be a plant expert; or be accompanied by one to pick anything. But I got into foraging by picking only familiar, easily identifiable species at first – nettles, blackberries, then wild garlic and three-cornered leek. The more I foraged, the more interested I became in other plants around me, and the more I noticed their unique characteristics.

When I take groups of younger school children foraging, I adapt the identification rule slightly to "Never eat anything that I can't positively identify". By this I mean that I always tell the children to show me anything that they are thinking of eating so that I can confirm, or not, their identification – there are some easy mistakes to make when foraging, such as confusing common sorrel (delicious, lemony leaf) with young Lords and Ladies (poisonous). I also tell them never to stick anything in their ear that's bigger than their elbow, but I'm not suggesting you adopt this rule as well.

Pollution

Don't pick from places that are likely to be contaminated, such as hedgerows next to busy roads, or farmland where pesticides or fertilisers have been used. Common sense is useful here – I normally tell children at school not to pick anything right next to a busy path if it is lower than the height of a dog's leg!

Permission

Make sure you have permission to pick if it is private land.

Quantity

Only take what you need, never more. I've found that children at Marlborough have developed a stronger sense of stewardship for their natural environment through foraging. By returning to the same spots, they've seen how different plants come and go with the seasons, and that this is only possible if these species are not completely removed.

Kids
in the
kitchen

Make having your kids in the kitchen with you as easy as possible by having a good routine set up.

Set aside a work surface that's at a suitable height for them to chop on, or a good solid chair for them to stand on. Cover the floor with something washable / disposable if this makes it easier. Know which knives you're happy for them to use.

Think of activities that are the right level for them and enough of a challenge to keep them interested. Have some back up solo activities planned that they can get on with if you need to sort out something hot, fiddly or sharp. Things like chopping herbs with scissors in a plastic jug or slicing some cucumber for dips are helpful for keeping them busy.

Remember to taste your food along the way and let your child join in with this. It's one of the most fun parts of cooking – the sneak preview. Ask your child what they think needs adding to improve the flavour (excluding chocolate)!

Let kids have some creative input into the meal; however small. Talk them through what you're doing. Even if it seems like they're not listening, they're probably absorbing more than you think.

Don't be afraid to let them get dirty. Children enjoy the textures of breading fish and taking the compost out. Once they get stuck in, they tend to forget that they were initially squeamish and are more likely to try dishes that they've had a hand in making.

Chopping

These holding and slicing methods are great, safe starting points for kids. Don't be afraid to let them use a knife, go slowly and calmly to start with. Our pupils grasp these methods and use them well, as they practise they gain confidence, speed and efficiency, but it does take time.

The bridge grip

The bridge grip method is the easiest for children and will help them cut things like tomatoes, peppers and bread (things you would usually use a serrated knife for).

Tomatoes are the best ingredient to practise on. You'll need a small serrated knife. Slice the tomatoes in half and place the flat bottom on the chopping board.

Grip the tomato as if you want to slide it side to side on the board, fingers on one edge, thumb on the opposite, gap between facing you, elbow sticking out to the side. Take the knife and use a sawing motion to slice through the tomato on the inside of your fingers. Move your fingers to the raw edge you've just sliced and repeat.

The claw grip

This is the basis of the method chefs use to chop their veg super fast! It's safe because your fingernails provide a smooth walled barrier between the knife and your fingers. With practise, you can move and chop along the object you're cutting in a seamless motion.

When chopping a potato using this method, slice it in half lengthways and place one half on its flat bottom. You'll need a sharp, straight edged knife as this technique uses the downward chopping motion rather than a sawing motion.

To begin, curl the fingers of the hand you don't chop with, and look at your fingernails. They should all be in a neat row. Place your clawed hand over the potato so the row of fingernails is at the edge at which you would like to begin slicing. Take the knife, and slice down. The side of the knife should brush past your fingers. When you've sliced, move the claw backwards to the thickness of slice you want and slice again. Repeat until the piece left is too small to slice any more.

Top tips

Always keep your knives sharp. Learning how to use a steel is the simplest way and older children can definitely do this. Working with sharp knives makes chopping easier, safer and a real pleasure.

The safest and easiest way to cut anything hard is on a stable, flat base. I often cut vegetables in half first to create a flat surface to rest on.

Consider using a wall mounted magnetic knife rack for storage. It's easy, hygienic and keeps knives sharp as they don't get bashed around in a drawer. When knives are displayed in a row like this, it's easier to explain to children which ones they can use, and which knives are used for which job.

Keeping clean in the kitchen

Remember to wash all your fruit and vegetables before use. The best way is to fill up a small sink or large bowl with warm water, put the produce in and give each piece a little scrub in the water with a vegetable scrubber before removing it. Some things are easier to wash after chopping, like leeks. We wash chopped leeks like we would lettuce leaves, in a sink full of fresh water. Leave them for a while, remove, drain the water then soak briefly in a second sinkful, making sure there is no grit left on the veg.

Tidying as you go in the kitchen makes cooking more relaxing and less chaotic; especially with kids around. If there are two of you, having someone on washing up duty while you're cooking makes the whole operation smoother.

Remember to teach your kids the importance of washing hands before getting started.

Kitchen equipment

Being a 'make do and mend' kind of person, I'm not going to suggest you need all the latest kitchen gadgets to cook fantastic, fresh and tasty food at home.

You don't. You can (and I often do, while out adventuring) get by with a set of billy pans, a knife, a chopping board and wooden spoon. So here's the happy midpoint between billy pans and flashy foodie paraphernalia – my essential kitchen kit.

Food processor

Without a food processor at school making our own hummus, curry pastes, pâtés or pestos would be out of the question as we just don't have time to crush things by hand. We also use it to dice large quantities of onion, garlic and carrots every day, which saves a lot of time and energy. I would recommend spending as much as you can afford on a quality brand. Try to get one with a slicing/ grating attachment as this can really speed up prep time and is safer for children to use (supervised) than a mandolin.

Mandolin

I am a huge fan of a mandolin. They can be a little intimidating as the blades are so sharp and with a harder vegetable like a squash it's easy to slip bladewards. Try using it with the finger guard. If you want to use it without, go very slowly at first, using soft vegetables like courgettes until you have the technique nailed. I mainly use the mandolin when I want vegetables sliced into very small sticks (julienne), so one step up from grated and a lot less soggy. We use a mandolin for our coleslaw and rosti recipes.

Knives

I use a good quality cooks' knife at school and at home. Keep it super-sharp and it'll cut anything, from crusty bread to cooked meat. I also use a small serrated knife for anything a little more fiddly, like slicing oranges (see our sherbert blood orange recipe on page 92) or slicing tomatoes.

Mixing bowls

I find my stainless steel nest of large to small mixing bowls very useful at home as they are lightweight, easy to store, and perhaps most importantly, easy to clean and dry. I like to use a big bowl for things like salads and coleslaws. More space allows you to really get things mixed up well without the annoying risk of things falling over the sides.

Trays

To be able to cook the recipes in Feed, you'll need a couple of flat, cookie type baking trays, and a couple of different sized deeper baking trays. A 20cm square is useful as is a 20cm x 30cm rectangular tray, along with some oven to table type ceramic dishes for things like pies and lasagnes.

Utensils

Aside from the obvious wooden spoons, spatulas, fish slice and tongs which all make cooking a lot easier, I would highly recommend investing in a good quality zester. Once you have used one of these, you will never want to use a spiky cheap version again. They're really easy to use, much safer for children and really enable you to make the most of whatever it is you are zesting. We use lemon zest a lot at school as a little flavour lifter added just before serving. I hate to see a lemon thrown away with its skin still intact – what a waste! It's also very useful to have a set of spoon measures and cup measures. I love my speed peeler, which is dead easy to use and really does speed up one of the less exciting kitchen chores.

Pans

Big pans, like big mixing bowls, are a great thing in the kitchen. Most things, I find, like to have space to cook in. Pasta, for instance, should be cooked in a really generous amount of boiling salted water, so that when the pasta is added it won't drop the temperature and hinder a continuous boil. A big saucepan, less than half full of sauce, lets you stir with vigour and ease, without the risk of overflow.

At school we use huge stock pans for most things, we can fry off 5kg of mince in one go and make 20 litres of soup. My pan essentials at home are:

★   A large, deep non stick frying pan for frying eggs, mushrooms, onions, garlic etc. Depth is good for making the transition into a sauce as it's a lot easier not to have to switch pans after sweating onions and garlic.

★   A large heavy-based saucepan or casserole pot (without plastic handles) with a lid for making soups, stews and slow cooking pasta sauces. This can also be popped straight into the oven.

★   A second large saucepan with lid for cooking pasta, rice and grains in lots of space.

★   For poaching eggs (something I do a lot at home) a medium heavy-based saucepan with a lid is good.

★   Scrambling eggs and warming things like tinned beans and chickpeas is best done in a small non-stick saucepan.

★   A good sized colander is handy, preferably one that can double as a steamer by fitting it inside your medium saucepan.

★   A heavy-based grill pan (aka cast iron griddle) is perfect for charring or cooking quickly without oil (like our flatbreads, on page 126). I love the smoky flavour that griddling meat or vegetables creates.

Main dishes – the whole shebang!

Smoked mackerel kedgeree

Serves 4 to 5

Start to finish ¾ hr
plus ½ hr to soak rice

—

Brown basmati rice
300g pre-soaked
for ½ hr

Eggs 4

Oil a glug

Large onion 1
peeled and sliced

Garam marsala 2 tsp

Turmeric 2 tsp

Cumin seeds 2 tsp

Ginger 1 thumb-size
peeled and finely diced

Garlic 3 cloves squashed,
peeled and diced

Shredded cabbage or
frozen peas, a handful

Lemon 1 juice and zest

Smoked mackerel fillets
300g bones and skin
removed and torn
into chunks

Greek-style yoghurt
a dollop per plate

**Coriander, pumpkin
seeds,pepper** and
lemon wedges to serve

The perfect combination of wholesome and delicious, this recipe brings together a few of my absolute favourite things – eggs, smoked fish, rice and spice. Smoked mackerel is a great fridge staple, as it works for snacks, is pretty cheap and packed with nutrients. Children really go for the nutty taste of brown basmati rice, so this quick hit dish is win-win.

1 — Drain your soaked rice and put into a medium saucepan with 450ml cold water. Cook with the lid on over a high heat until it boils, then turn it down to a simmer. The water will be fully absorbed during cooking so stir only once throughout. After about 20 minutes, when cooked through, take the rice off the heat and remove the lid. **2** — Boil a medium saucepan of water, add the eggs to the water and simmer for around 8 minutes depending on the size of your eggs. **3** — Remove the eggs and stick them under running cold water until cool. **4** — Meanwhile, warm your oil, in a large non-stick frying pan, throw in the onions and let them sweat for a couple of minutes before adding the spices, garlic and ginger. Give everything a good stir and wait until things start to smell fragrant before adding your veg. Stir well and leave to cook through for a couple of minutes. **5** — Peel the eggs and slice into quarters, set aside to pop on top at the end. **6** — Add the cooked rice to the onion spice mix. Stir through with the lemon zest and juice, ensuring the rice takes on a golden colour throughout. Stir through the smoked mackerel. When everything is piping hot, you're ready to go! **7** — In a wide bowl or plate, serve your rice and fish, top with egg quarters, a dollop of yoghurt, chopped fresh coriander, a lemon wedge each and a sprinkle of pumpkin seeds and pepper.

Serves 4 to 5

Start to finish 2 to 3 hrs to boil the ham ½ hr to make soup

—

Ham hock 1 soaked overnight in water in the fridge

Bay leaves 2

Peppercorns 1 tsp

Leeks 3, outer leaves separated from white insides, all washed and roughly chopped

Garlic cloves 2 peeled and chopped

Carrot 1 peeled and roughly chopped

Olive oil 1 tbsp

Potato 1 chopped into small 1cm cubes, no need to peel

Frozen peas 500g

Parsley half a bunch of fresh leaves picked and chopped

Basil half a bunch of fresh basil, chopped, stalks and all

Lemon 1 zest and juice

1 — Rinse the soaked ham hock and place it in a large lidded pan. Cover with cold water and bring to the boil over a medium heat. **2** — Add the bay leaves, peppercorns, outer leaves of leek, garlic cloves, carrot and onion. Give it all a good mix and when it comes to the boil, turn it down to a simmer, leaving for 2–3 hours, stirring occasionally. The ham is ready when the meat comes easily away from the bone. **3** — Remove the hock from the liquid and leave to cool until you can safely shred the meat away from the bone. **4** — Don't throw away the liquid, this is your delicious pork stock. Drain it through a colander into another pan and if you are making the soup straight away, put it over a low heat. Taste it to check it's not too salty, soaking the ham hock should have eliminated excess salt, but better to be safe than sorry! If it is too salty, substitute for vegetable stock or boiling water when making the soup **5** — When you are ready to make your soup, sauté the remaining parts of the leeks and the potato over a low heat with a little olive oil. When the leeks are soft, juicy and sweet, add a litre of your pork stock. **6** — Let the mixture come up to a very gentle simmer for around 5 minutes and then add your peas. Give the mix another 5 minutes and then add the fresh chopped herbs and take off the heat. **7** — Blitz with a hand held stick blender. Taste the soup before seasoning. A twist of pepper and a squirt of lemon juice. **8** — Stir through the shredded ham hock, leaving some to garnish the top, along with another grind or two of pepper and the lemon zest.

★ *If you struggle to find a ham hock but really want to make the soup (we don't blame you) then substitute the hock for a small gammon joint, soak and boil it exactly the same way.*

Ham, leek and pea soup

Ham hock is the piggy's ankle. It's not fatty but likes a really long boil to make it tender. Hocks are best sourced from farm shops, butchers and direct from good pork farmers.

Cauliflower and kale macaroni cheese

This is a great recipe for pasta lovers and cauliflower sceptics, most of whom can't help but like it when smothered in a rich cheese sauce. Our local organic farm's kale and cauliflower are my favourite, as I know they're field-fresh.

1 — Heat at least 2 litres of salted water in the biggest pan you have, as you'll also be adding both pasta and veg to this pan. **2** — Preheat your oven to 190°C / gas mark 5 and get a large oven-proof dish ready. **3** — Melt the butter in a non-stick saucepan over a medium heat. **4** — Add the flour and whisk vigorously to form a paste, let this paste cook for a couple of minutes before starting to trickle in your milk, stirring ALL the time! Keep stirring and trickling the milk until all is added (a little helper can be useful at this stage). The sauce will become wonderfully thick and creamy. **5** — Switch to a wooden spoon (preferably square edged, to get into the corners of the pan) and let the sauce slowly bubble for a few minutes. **6** — Turn off the heat, add black pepper and grate in some nutmeg to taste. **7** — Tip in about ¾ of the cheese, leaving the rest for the topping and stir. Taste to see if it's cheesy enough, peppery enough and nutmeggy enough for your liking. **8** — In the meantime, add the pasta to the pan of boiling water, pop the lid back on and then a few minutes before it's done, add the cauliflower and kale. Drain it all when the pasta is al dente. If the cauliflower is still a little hard, don't worry, it will continue cooking in the oven. **9** — Mix your pasta and veg with your sauce, tip into your tray and sprinkle with cheese and then the handful of breadcrumbs. Bake for 20 minutes until the cheese is bubbling and golden on top.

Serves 4 to 5

Start to finish ¾ hr

—

Butter 100g

Flour 100g

Milk 1 litre

Black pepper and **Nutmeg** to taste

Mature cheddar 2 grated handfuls, remember to leave some for the topping

Macaroni 500g or other pasta of your choice

Cauliflower 600g chopped into small pieces about the size of a sprout

Fresh kale 200g washed and shredded

Fresh breadcrumbs a handful (optional)

Luscious lamb and coconut curry

This is a delicious, mild but flavoursome curry – a perfect way to use a cheaper cut of lamb. Cook this long and slow and serve with turmeric rice and green veg for a bright rainbow plate. Curries are great if you have a little bit of time one day to get ahead for the week. The flavours will deepen if left in the fridge for a day or so before reheating.

Serves 4 to 5

Start to finish ½ hr prep, 2–3 hrs bubbling away

—

Onions 1 roughly chopped

Garlic cloves 2 crushed and peeled

ginger a thumb-sized piece, peeled

Oil a glug

Stewing lamb 500g chopped into 2cm pieces

Cumin 1 tbsp

Ground coriander 1 tsp

Turmeric 1 tsp

Cinnamon ½ tsp

Garam marsala 1 tsp

Salt 1 tsp

Creamed coconut or thick coconut milk 150g

Chopped tomatoes 400g can

Greek yoghurt a big spoonful (optional)

1 — Blitz the onions, garlic and fresh ginger to a paste with a couple of tablespoons of water in a food processor before starting the cooking, set paste aside. **2** — Then warm oil and brown the lamb pieces in a large heavy bottomed pan or casserole dish for around 10 minutes, stirring to ensure they turn golden on all sides. The pan should build up a lovely brown sticky coating on the bottom, which is great for building up the curry's flavour. **3** — Add the spices and salt and cook, stirring for a few more minutes until the contents become fragrant and smell delicious. **4** — Add the coconut cream, the onion paste you made earlier and the tomatoes, give everything a good stir and bring it down to a gentle simmer. **5** — Pop a lid on and turn the heat down to low so it bubbles away gently. Leave, stirring from time to time, for a couple of hours until the meat is soft. If the sauce looks a little wet, remove the lid and turn up the heat a bit, as this will reduce it slightly. If it's a bit dry, add some water or liquid from the coconut milk. **6** — When the meat is soft and tender and the sauce is reduced and thick, your curry is ready. If you would like to make it creamier, stir in the spoonful of yoghurt, once off the heat.

★ *To spice this curry up, add some diced fresh chillies at the beginning with the spices, the more you add, the hotter it gets!*

Curried parsnip soup

Serves 4 to 5

Start to finish ¾ hr

—

Oil a glug

Onions 1
roughly chopped

Turmeric Powder 2 tsp

Garam Masala 2 tsp

Cumin seeds 1 tsp

Ginger a thumb of
ginger, chopped

Garlic cloves 2 peeled

Cardamom 1½ tsp
or 2 squashed pods

Potatoes 2 small
scrubbed and
roughly diced

Parsnips 3 large
scrubbed and roughly
chopped into even
rounds

Vegetable stock 1 litre
or bouillon made to
packet instructions

Coconut milk 400ml tin

Yogurt and
chilli to serve

Really tasty, fresh and organic parsnips will make this easy recipe really sing; from October onwards they're abundant in the UK so you should find them to be good value. I always buy organic spices – the price difference per use is really nothing at all so I always make the investment.

1 — Throw all your vegetables, garlic, ginger and spices into a large heavy-based pan with the glug of olive oil and warm them gently over a low heat until the vegetables start to go soft and you can smell the spices. **2** — Add the stock and coconut milk, stick a lid on and wait for the mix to come up to a simmer. **3** — Keep it slowly simmering for around 25 minutes, until your parsnip and potato are both soft. **4** — Take the soup off the heat and blitz until smooth using a hand held stick blender. **5** — Pop back on the heat to keep warm until ready to serve. **6** — Serve in deep bowls with a swirl of yoghurt and a sprinkle of chilli flakes.

Warming beef and butternut stew

This warming, hearty stew is a perfect autumnal meal for family and friends to share. Hot-pot style dishes are great for weekend cook-ups to ease you into a busy week. Great with a steaming bowl of mash and greens or try dunking in fresh sliced baguette.

1 — Dice the onions, celery and carrots. Peel and chop the butternut squash into bite-sized chunks. **2** — Fry the bacon bits over a medium heat in a large heavy bottomed pan or casserole dish until they crisp up. Remove from the pan, ready to throw back in later. **3** — Tip the diced beef into a large bowl and coat with the flour. Pop the beef in the casserole dish and brown over a medium heat. Then remove the meat from the pan and leave to rest with the bacon for a minute whilst you start off your vegetables. **4** — Throw the onion, celery and carrots into the casserole dish, sweat over a low heat, adding a glug of olive oil if it starts to look a little dry. The meat should have browned the bottom of the pan. **5** — When the veg has softened, add the meat and give everything a good stir. Then add the hot stock and chopped tomatoes. **6** — Bring your stew to the boil, pop the lid on and turn the heat right down. Now either keep cooking on the stove or, if you're using a casserole dish, put it in the oven at 150°C / gas mark 2. Cook for 2 hours. **7** — After an hour and a half, add your diced squash and give it a good stir before returning to the oven. **8** — When the beef is soft and melty, taste the sauce for seasoning and, if it needs it, add a dash of balsamic vinegar for sweetness, add the peas if using and leave for just a few minutes to let them heat through.

Serves 4 to 5

Start to finish ½ hr plus 1 hr slow cooking

—

Oil a glug

Good quality bacon 100g diced

Good quality beef shin 500g diced

Flour 1 tbsp

Onions 2 diced

Celery 3 sticks diced

Carrots 3 scrubbed and diced

Chopped rosemary 1 tsp

Fresh thyme 1 tsp picked

Chopped tomatoes 400g tin

Chicken or vegetable stock 500ml

Butternut squash 1 small, peeled and chopped into bitesize chunks

Balsamic vinegar a dash

Fresh or **frozen peas** 1 handful (optional)

Fancy pants smoked salmon pasta

Serves 4 to 5

Start to finish ½ hr

—

Oil a glug

Onion 1 peeled
and sliced

Garlic 2 chopped cloves

Fennel bulb 1 large
washed and sliced

White sauce a batch
(see page 134)

Smoked salmon 120g
trimmings or sliced
pieces

Crème fraîche
1 heaped tbsp

Dried pasta 500g

Podded peas handful
of frozen/fresh

A lemon zest and **juice**

Salt and **pepper**

Fragrant, elegant and sumptuous, this fishy dish works as well for a big lunch with friends as it does for a school dinner for two hundred children. The fennel really enlivens the flavours and textures and the dish is very easy to make.

1 — Boil a large saucepan of salted water with the lid on for your pasta. **2** — Meanwhile, add a glug of olive oil in a large frying pan and start to fry the onions, garlic and fennel over a low heat until they softened and turn golden. Be careful they don't catch – we're aiming for caramelised not burnt! **3** — Make up a white sauce (see page 134), add the smoked salmon slices and the crème fraîche and keep it bubbling away on the lowest heat, making sure you stir from time to time. **4** — When the pasta pan comes to a rolling boil, add your pasta and cook, following the directions on your packet. Add the peas 5 minutes before the end of cooking. Once it's done, drain and keep some water aside to loosen the sauce. **5** — When everything's ready, combine it all in the large pasta pan, stir well and add some saved pasta water to loosen if needed. **6** — Top off with the lemon zest and juice and then season to taste.

★ *Little fingers are perfect for podding peas and if you make this in the summer months I really recommend going the extra mile and buying fresh. Unzip the pod by pulling the stem from the top and backwards, the stringy bit should pull down, unlocking the little peas inside.*

Sweet beet halloumi burgers

Makes 8 burgers

Start to finish ¾ hr plus ½ hr soaking time

—

Beetroot 4 medium or 5 small peeled and grated

Halloumi 200g grated

Porridge oats 150g (to substitute jumbo oats, blitz them down in a food processor before using)

Onion 1 small peeled and diced by hand or food processor

Garlic 2 cloves minced

Extra virgin olive oil 2 tbsp

Eggs 2 large

Olive oil a drizzle

A friend cooked me a burger like this once when we were both working on a farm in Italy. I was working in the kitchen, she was outdoors, but we both learned a whole heap of stuff about their food which the locals there were so rightly very proud of and connected to. I thought these burgers were worth recreating when I started at the school, incorporating one of my favourite cheeses to balance the sweet beetroot.

1 — Weigh, peel, grate and blitz all your ingredients. **2** — Mix everything together in a large bowl, with your hands. Why not get the kids to do this messy job? Don't get caught pink handed though – wash your hands straight after mixing. **3** — Set the mix aside to soak for half an hour. **4** — Preheat your oven to 200°C / gas mark 6. **5** — Separate the mix out into 8 parts and shape into burgers. Place burgers on a tray and drizzle with olive oil. **6** — Bake in the oven for around 20 minutes, giving them a flip at half time. **7** — Serve sandwiched in a bun with a dollop of our tzatziki (see page 69) and some sliced cucumber and crunchy lettuce.

★ *No beetroot in the house? Try swapping them for carrots, the recipe works just as well with lovely orange carrots!*

Cauliflower cheese soup

Smooth, decedent and velvety, this soup feels like a real treat but is actually made from the most humble ingredients – cauliflower, milk and stale bread!

1 — Prepare your vegetables and melt the butter in a heavy-based saucepan over a medium heat. Add the onions, garlic, salt and cauliflower and cook them all for around ten minutes, stirring all the time, until the veg is soft and starting to brown. **2** — Add the bouillon powder and give it a stir around, then add the milk. **3** — Warm the milk gently to ensure it doesn't boil; let it simmer away for around ten minutes before adding the bread. This will thicken the soup. Take it off the heat and leave for a couple of minutes before adding your cheese and then blitzing with a stick hand blender. Add boiling water until you reach the desired consistency. Stir in the mustard and nutmeg and taste for seasoning, you may want to add some pepper. **4** — I like this served with a scattering of toasted walnut and chopped parsley, along with some hot buttery toast.

★ *Why not try swapping the cheddar for your favourite blue cheese? A crumbly Cornish Blue would really give this soup some extra muscles!*

Serves 4 to 5 with enough for lunch leftovers the next day

Start to finish ¾ hr

—

Onions 2 peeled and roughly sliced

Garlic 2 cloves, squashed and peeled

Salt 1 tsp

Cauliflower 2 heads (1kg), washed and broken into florets then halved, with stalk diced

Vegetable bouillon powder 1 tbsp

Whole milk 1 litre

Good quality stale bread 1 handful in chunks

Mature cheddar 2 grated handfuls

Wholegrain mustard 1½ tbsp

Nutmeg a good grating

Pepper to taste

Parsley and **toasted walnuts** to serve (optional)

Happy homity pies

Once you've learnt how to quickly make these little pastry cups they can be used for a whole host of pies; sweet or savoury. Serve with lots of veg and salad to lighten up what can otherwise be a slightly cream and carb heavy dish.

Makes 12 child
sized pies

Start to finish 1 hr

—

Puff pastry 400g of
our cheats' puff pastry
(see page 135)

Potato 500g mashed,
leftovers are perfect

Double cream a splash

Wholegrain mustard
1 tbsp

Spring onions a bunch
washed, trimmed and
sliced thinly

Mature cheddar cheese
a handful grated plus
a little for sprinkling
the tops

Salt and **pepper** to taste

1 — Prepare a 12 hole muffin tin and roll out your pastry on a well-floured surface to about the thickness of a pound coin, cut 12 circles, using a circle cutter that's 1 or 2 centimetres bigger than the holes on your muffin tin. **2** — Press each circle down into each hole of the muffin tin to make a little cup, no need to grease, there will be some overlap that you just need to press gently together with your finger. Once you have completed the tray, stick it in the freezer for 10 minutes or so whilst you prepare 12 15cm squares of baking paper, scrunching each one a couple of times to make it flexible and lose its sharp edges. Rope the kids in to help with this. These squares can be reused next time. Preheat oven to 200°C / gas mark 6. **3** — Remove the muffin tray from the freezer, and pop a paper square in each cup and fill with baking beans. Bake in the oven for 10 minutes until the pastry cup is golden and crisp and the paper cup can be easily removed with the beans inside. Remove the paper cups and beans then leave for a few minutes to cool slightly before lifting the pastry cups gently out and placing onto a lined flat baking tray. **4** — Whilst blind-baking your pies, you can be getting the filling ready, which is just a case of mixing all remaining ingredients together in a big bowl and tasting to see if it needs more cheese or pepper. **5** — When your pastry cups are ready, turn your oven down to 180°C / gas mark 4 and pile the mix into the cups, you want it to be mound-like in appearance. Sprinkle some more cheddar carefully over the top of each pie and pop in the oven for around 15 minutes, until piping hot all the way through. **6** — Serve hot, warm or even cold!

Serves 4 to 5

Start to finish 1½ hrs

—

Squash 1 large
crown prince or
butternut squash

Fresh picked thyme
1 tbsp

Sage leaves
1 tbsp chopped

Oil a glug

Salt and **pepper**

Garlic cloves 2 large
crushed, peeled

White sauce 1 batch
(see page 134)

Cheddar 250g grated

Onions 2 peeled and
sliced thinly

Fresh thyme leaves
1 tbsp

Red peppers
2 sliced thinly

Cherry tomatoes 500g
fresh or a 400g tin of
chopped tomatoes

White wine a splash

Fresh spinach leaves
250g

Goats cheese 400g

Lasagne sheets 250g

1 — Preheat oven to 180°C / gas mark 4. **2** — Chop the squash into quarters and remove seeds, no need to peel. Place on a roasting tray, big enough to hold the pieces snugly. Sprinkle over the chopped thyme and sage, a drizzle of olive oil and nestle in the garlic halves. Season with salt and pepper, then bake in the oven for around 25 minutes until the squash is soft. **3** — Meanwhile, prepare a batch of white sauce (we show you how on page 134). Add half the grated cheese, cover and set aside. **4** — Heat up a large deep frying pan, then add a glug of olive oil and your prepared onions and peppers. Let them cook on a medium heat whilst stirring for a couple of minutes until they soften, then add the whole cherry tomatoes or tinned tomatoes. After a couple of minutes turn up the heat and add the wine and the spinach. Give it a good stir, so the spinach becomes submerged, and when the liquid has bubbled away a little, turn off the heat. Season to taste and set aside. **5** — Remove the tray of squash from the oven and let it cool until you can handle it enough to scrape the flesh from the skins. Discard the skins and then mash the squash together with the herbs and garlic and fold through the goat's cheese. **6** — Time to build. You will need a deep oven tray around 30cm x 20cm. Start with a layer of the tomato sauce, use half of it, and spread it out to cover the bottom of the tin. Next add a layer of lasagne sheets, pressing them down as you do. It's the squash layer next, add half of it and flatten it evenly across the lasagne sheets, before pouring over a layer of white sauce. Add another layer of lasagne sheets, again press them down, then the remainder of your tomato sauce, the rest of your squash, and the final layer of lasagne sheets, the rest of the white sauce and a sprinkling of cheddar and black pepper to finish. **7** — Bake in the oven for 30–45 minutes, until it's piping hot in the centre and the lasagne sheets feel soft when poked with a knife.

Squash and goats cheese lasagne

One for the weekend, this recipe is great for getting lasagne-loving kids into deliciously sweet and wholesome squash and is well worth a bit of effort to put together. We like to use Crown Prince squash for this recipe, they grow so well in Cornwall and have a really special flavour. They keep for ages, so never turn one down at a roadside produce stall.

Crispy breaded mackerel

Mackerel in season is such good value and a great way to turn kids on to the pleasures of oily fish. Make life a bit easier for yourself by getting your local fishmonger to gut, wash and fillet these tasty little morsels. Some say that you shouldn't freeze fresh mackerel because of flavour loss and mushiness, but we do and they taste like they've just been reeled in. Kids love these crispy fillets rolled up in wraps with salad and mayo, though they also make a delicious snack for peckish parents straight from the fridge.

1 — Check your fillets for any larger bones (the tiny bones are fine to eat). Fins can simply be pulled out or chopped off. **2** — Prepare a baking tray with a light coating of olive oil and preheat your oven to 180°C / gas mark 4 or switch your grill on. **3** — Set up your three dipping stations: a dish of whisked egg, a dish of flour, and one dish of breadcrumbs mixed with lemon zest. **4** — Mix a little salt and pepper into the flour. **5** — Take your mackerel fillet and coat it first with flour, then egg, then breadcrumbs and then lay it onto the oiled tray. A word of warning here, prepare to get messy! **6** — Drizzle a little olive oil over the fish. **7** — If you're grilling, these tiny fish should only take a couple of minutes on each side. If you've opted to oven cook, bake the fillets for 5–10 minutes on each side, depending on size. **8** — Squeeze some lemon juice over these deliciously crisp and golden fish and enjoy!

Serves 4 to 5 with enough for lunch leftovers the next day

Start to finish ¾ hr

—

Fresh Mackerel 10 fillets, cut down either side of central pinbones on each fillet to make two long pieces

Oil a drizzle

Eggs 2

Flour a handful

Breadcrumbs 300g

Lemon 1 zested and halved

Salt and **pepper**

★ *We also use this method to bread sardine fillets, it works just as well and although they're probably a little bit harder to find; they're even cheaper! When you see them, snap them up!*

Stack 'em up savoury pancakes

Serves 4 to 5

Start to finish ½ hr

—

Plain flour 100g

Baking powder 1½ tsp

Salt 1 tsp

Eggs 3

Sweetcorn 300g

Spring onions 4 washed and sliced

Red pepper 1 washed, stalks removed and diced

Oil 1 tbsp for frying

These are such fun to make and a real family favourite. A great balance of sweet and savoury, serve these pancakes as a healthy snack or transform into a quick and tasty meal by serving with tomato salsa, fresh chopped avocado and rice.

1 — Blitz the flour, baking powder, salt, eggs, half the sweetcorn and half of the chopped spring onions in a food processor until you have a smoothish batter with no flour lumps. **2** — Put the mixture in a bowl and stir in the remaining sweetcorn, sliced spring onions and diced red pepper. **3** — When ready to eat (the mix can be left for a couple of hours in the fridge), warm the oil in a non-stick frying pan, and when the pan is nice and hot, ladle in the mix, about 2 tbsp at a time, letting them form rough rounds. You should be able to fit four or five rounds in a large frying pan at once. **4** — When the edges of the pancakes look dry and bubbles rise through them, they're ready to flip. **5** — Cook them until they are crisp and golden on both sides and enjoy them best fresh from the pan!

★ *Give these pancakes a chilli kick by adding half a teaspoon of chilli flakes to the mix in step one.*

Pasta con le sarde

This is a pasta dish to quickly rustle up next time you see sardines for sale, everyone loves this tomato-y sweet and sour sauce, perfectly complemented by the rich oily fish and garlicky crispy crumb topping. If you can't find fresh sardines, use well sourced tinned sardines, tuna or mackerel as a substitute.

Serves 4 to 5

Start to finish ½ hr

—

Olive oil a large glug

Onion 1

Red chilli 1 sliced (optional, but delicious)

Cloves garlic 3 peeled and minced

Capers 1 tbsp

Passata 700g jar

Bay leaf 1

Honey 1 tsp

Balsamic vinegar a splash

Dried pasta 500g

Sardine fillets 200g checked through for large bones/fins

Fresh breadcrumbs a handful

Garlic oil 1 tsp

Fresh parsley a handful chopped

1 — Bring a large pan of salted water to the boil for your pasta. **2** — Meanwhile warm a large deep frying pan over a medium heat with a glug of olive oil. Add the diced onion, chilli and garlic and stir for around 10 minutes until soft. **3** — Tip in the whole jar of passata. Give the jar a shake with a bit of water inside and add this too. **4** — Drizzle in the balsamic and honey, add the capers and the bay leaf and let the sauce simmer. **5** — Cook your pasta, using the packet instructions for timings. **6** — Once your pasta is on, stir the sardine fillets into the sauce. They'll cook through quite quickly and break up into the sauce. **7** — Taste your sauce, sweeten it up with a dash more honey or balsamic, and, if you like, add a pinch of pepper. **8** — Time to begin your crispy breadcrumb topping. Heat a small frying pan with a glug of garlic oil and throw in your breadcrumbs. Let the crumbs fry until crisp, then take off the heat and stir in the chopped parsley. **9** — By now your pasta should be al dente and ready to drain. Save some water to loosen the sauce if you need to. **10** — Add the pasta to the pan full of sauce, give everything a good mix over the heat. Dish it up and top with the crispy crumb topping.

★ *We've used garlic oil for our crispy crumb topping in this recipe. It's really easy to make your own garlic oil, just crush and peel around five fat cloves and pop them in a clean 500ml bottle. Top up with your favourite olive oil and leave for a week or so, shaking from time to time before you use it.*

Cheesy leek pasties

Starting with a batch of good pastry is the key to this recipe. Oh, and a good, strong cheese. We make mini pasties at school and serve with veggies and rice, but these pasties also make great picnic food.

1 — Start by melting the butter in a deep frying pan warmed over a medium heat. Throw in the onions, potato, leeks and thyme and cook, stirring from time to time for 5 minutes until the potato has softened. **2** — Add the mustard and crème fraîche and give it all a good stir up. Remove from the heat and crumble in the grated cheese. Season to taste and then leave to cool slightly whilst rolling the pastry. **3** — Preheat the oven to 190°C / gas mark 5 and find a couple of flat trays. **4** — Break the egg into a small bowl, adding the dash of milk and mixing with a fork until smooth. This is your egg wash, which is brushed over the pastry to make it shiny when it comes out of the oven. **5** — Roll out your pastry so it's about the thickness of a pound coin. Use a circle cutter or empty tin to press out circles. Squash your pastry bits together and reroll until it's all used up – any scraps can be cut into fun shapes and baked alongside. **6** — Place a couple of spoons of leek mix inside the circle, weighted towards one half. Brush around the edge with the egg wash and fold the emptier half over the top, sealing with your fingers along the edge to form a pasty parcel. Crimp if you like or press with a fork if you prefer. Place onto a baking tray and brush the pasty with the egg wash. Prod the top with a fork to create some little steam holes. Repeat to make all the pasties. **7** — Bake for about 20 minutes, until they are crackly and golden on top and piping hot in the centre.

Makes 8 to 10 kid's size pasties

Start to finish 1 hr

—

Butter a knob

Onion 1 peeled and diced

Potatoes 2 medium scrubbed, no need to peel, quartered and then sliced thinly

Leeks 3 cleaned, halved and sliced at 1cm intervals

Fresh thyme leaves 1 tsp

Wholegrain mustard 1 tbsp

Crème fraîche 100g

Mature cheddar 100g grated

Puff pastry 2x 400g of our cheat's puff pastry (see page 135)

Egg 1

Milk a dash

Spicy keema beef

Serves 4 to 5

Start to finish ¾ hr

—

Potatoes 300g (2–3)
all-rounder scrubbed
and diced into small
cubes, no need to peel

Oil a glug

Onion 1 peeled
and diced

Turmeric 2 tsp

Garam marsala 2 tsp

Ground coriander 1 tsp

Cumin seeds 2 tsp

Mustard seeds 1 tsp
yellow or brown

Beef mince 500g

Frozen peas a handful

**Julienned/grated
carrot** 200g (2–3)

Pickled chillies
(see page 70)

Natural yoghurt and
coriander to serve

This is a real fuss free and fast cook up for a cosy winter night in, a spicy twist on those all familiar and much loved ingredients: mince, potatoes, peas and carrots. Mince is great because it's so affordable, even organic beef mince won't break the bank. Speed this one up even more; skip the potatoes and start with step three.

1 — Pop the potatoes into a medium saucepan of cold water and bring to the boil. **2** — Simmer until cooked through, then drain, leaving the potatoes in a colander over the pan to dry out. **3** — Meanwhile, pour a glug of oil into a large frying pan and fry the onions over a low heat. **4** — When the onions start to soften and turn golden, scatter in the spices and continue stirring for a few minutes, until they start to smell fragrant. **5** — Add the mince and break it up with a wooden spoon while it's cooking. Brown all over and cook through. **6** — Add the peas, the julienned or grated carrot and the potatoes and give everything a good stir. Cook on for about ten minutes until everything is piping hot. **7** — Sprinkle with pickled chillies and roughly chopped coriander then serve with rice and a dollop of natural yoghurt.

★ *Any little helpers around? Get them dicing your potatoes into perfect cubes, grating your carrots or measuring out your spices.*

Store cupboard tomato and sesame soup

Serves 4 to 5

Start to finish ½ hr

—

Onion 1 peeled and roughly chopped

Garlic 2 cloves peeled and squished

Olive oil glug

Tomatoes 2 tins of good quality chopped or whole fresh

Miso paste 1 heaped tbsp

Bouillon powder 1 heaped tbsp or a veggie stock cube

Boiling water 500ml

Tahini 1 heaped tbsp

Sesame seeds and **chopped coriander** to garnish

This soup comes together so quickly but has such an interesting and comforting flavour; I hoped the children would love it and they absolutely do. This is our version of the soup which we make through the winter; it uses almost only store cupboard ingredients which we find really helpful some days.

1 — Prepare the onion and garlic, sweat over a low heat in a heavy bottomed saucepan until they've begun to soften and smell sweet. **2** — Meanwhile boil the kettle and place the miso and bouillon powder in a heatproof jug. Stir in around 500ml of boiling water until all is dissolved. **3** — Add the tinned tomatoes to the pan along with the miso stock. Cover and let it simmer slowly for around 10 minutes. **4** — Take off the heat and blitz until smooth with a handheld stick blender. Add the tahini paste and stir until dissolved, taste for seasoning. **5** — Serve with fresh sourdough bread or our spinach cheese straws (page 120) to dunk, topped with a sprinkle of sesame seeds and some fresh herbs.

★ *Super flavoursome smooth soups like ours can double up as sauces, so why not warm up any leftovers and pour them over anything that needs a bit of something on top the next day?*

Turkey and courgette burgers

Makes 10 small burgers

Start to finish ¾ hr

—

Turkey mince 500g

Courgettes 2 weighing around 200g in total, washed and grated on the mandolin or on a box grater

Breadcrumbs a handful of fresh or frozen

Egg 1

Lemon zest of 1

Garlic 1 clove of chopped, or 1 tsp garlic paste

Oregano a heaped tsp

Salt and **pepper** pinch (to taste)

This ever popular recipe is one for the kids to take care of; all they will need is some supervision using the oven. These burgers are also perfect for the BBQ, pop them into the fridge to firm up beforehand.

1 — Line a baking sheet with baking paper and warm the grill. **2** — Using a large mixing bowl, combine all the ingredients with your hands, until you have a sticky mix that will form easily into patty shapes. **3** — To test your flavours, warm a frying pan with a little drip of oil and drop in a small amount of mix. Fry for a couple of minutes on either side until cooked through. Taste for seasoning; if the mix needs a little salt, pepper or garlic add accordingly. **4** — Once you are happy with the taste, form into patties of desired size and pop onto tray. **5** — Grill for around 10 minutes on both sides until they are golden brown and piping hot all the way through. **6** — Serve as you like, we like them in buns, with lettuce, tomato and hummus (see page 68).

★ *Switch it up by stirring a couple of tablespoons of green pesto into the mix instead of the garlic, lemon and oregano. Our really wild garlic pesto on page 73 would be perfect for the job!*

★ *Courgettes are perfect for growing at home, they grow really happily in pots on the patio as well as in the ground; sow seeds indoors in the winter then plant out after the last threat of frost has passed.*

Monday night's chicken pie

This is a perfect way to use leftover roast chicken, in a dish that tastes like anything but leftovers. Serve with greens or a simple garden salad and our baked sweet potato fries on page 117.

1 — Preheat oven to 180°C / gas mark 4 and choose a pie dish around 30cm in diameter. 2 — Pour the milk into a saucepan set over a low heat, scattering in the bay leaves. Turn off the heat as soon as you see the promise of bubbles. 3 — Meanwhile, warm a heavy bottomed large casserole-type pan and melt the knob of butter. Fry your bacon pieces until they start to crisp up, then add all the vegetables, the thyme leaves and the garlic and stir over a low heat for around 10 minutes to soften. 4 — Stir in the flour so that it coats all the vegetables and cook for a few minutes before slowly adding the milk, stirring all the while. 5 — When you've added all of your milk, add the chicken and let the mix thicken whilst stirring. When it starts to thicken, let it bubble away for a few minutes and then stir in the spinach, sweetcorn and parsley and take off the heat. Season well. 6 — Pour mix into your chosen pie dish and unroll the filo pastry onto a clean work surface; pour the 50g of oil or melted butter into a small ramekin. 7 — Pop a layer of filo over the pie contents, tucking it in around the sides, brush with butter and then another layer, carrying on, remembering to brush butter or oil between each layer. You can scrunch some filo layers up, it looks nice to do this on the top layer, giving it a really crinkly rustic look. Finish the pie with a brushing of butter or oil and pop into the oven. 8 — Bake for 30 minutes until the pastry is crisp and the filling is piping hot.

Serves 4 to 5

Start to finish 1¼ hrs

—

Milk 500ml

Bay leaves 2 peeled and roughly sliced

Butter a knob

Good quality bacon 3 rashers sliced thinly

Carrot 1 scrubbed and diced into 1cm cubes

Onion 1 medium peeled and diced

Large waxy potato 1 (around 300g) scrubbed and diced into 1cm cubes

Fresh thyme leaves handful picked from the stalks

Garlic 2 cloves crushed peeled and diced

Flour 2 heaped tbsp

Roasted chicken 300g torn into pieces

Fresh spinach leaves 100g

Sweetcorn 1 handful either frozen, tinned or the kernels sliced from a fresh cob

Fresh parsley a handful chopped

Salt and **pepper**

Filo pastry 8–10 sheets

Butter 50g melted or **olive oil**

Saffron squid stew

Serves 4 to 5

Start to finish ½ hr prep plus 2 hrs slow cooking

—

Olive oil a glug

Onions 2 peeled and sliced thinly

Fennel 1 bulb scrubbed and chopped roughly

Garlic 2 cloves peeled and thinly sliced

Smoked paprika 2 tbsp

Fennel seeds 1 tsp

Chopped tomatoes 2 x 400g tins

Bay leaves 2

Saffron a large pinch soaked in a splash of boiling water

Squid 500g cleaned chopped into rings and similar sized pieces

New potatoes a large handful, chopped

Lemon 3 slices

White fish fillets 400g skinned, boned and chopped into chunks

Fresh mussels 500g scrubbed and debearded, any open ones discarded

Flat leaf parsley a handful of fresh roughly chopped to garnish

Slow cooking squid gives it a tender, chicken-like bite and infuses this stew with the sweet and salty taste of the sea. Smoky paprika and saffron give this dish a warming Mediterranean feel.

1 — Begin by warming a large glug of olive oil in a heavy bottomed pan or casserole dish. Chuck in your prepared veg and stir over a medium heat for a few minutes before adding the paprika, fennel seeds and bay. Keep stirring and cook until the veg is soft and spices are fragrant. **2** — Add the tomatoes, the saffron in its liquor and the cleaned and chopped squid and fill your two tomato cans full of water and add those too. Wait for the pan to come up to a boil and then turn it right down to a gentle simmer. Stir from time to time over the next couple of hours until the squid is tender – it'll lose all its chewiness. Add the chopped new potatoes about an hour into the time. **3** — While that's bubbling away prepare the rest of your fish and mussels. **4** — When you're just about ready to serve, throw in the fish, the lemon slices and mussels. They'll only take a couple of minutes to cook. Gently stir them through the sauce (keeping them intact). Spoon into bowls and serve with fresh buttered crusty bread and a scattering of fresh chopped parsley.

Makes 4 medium pizzas

Start to finish 1 hr plus proving

—

BASE

Water 350ml lukewarm

Fast action dried yeast 7g sachet

Sugar 1 tsp

Olive oil 2 tbsp

Flour 500g strong white or a mix of strong white and wholemeal

Salt ½ tsp

—

TOPPING

Tomato sauce ½ batch of our tomato sauce (page 136) or a 700g jar of passata

Mozzarella 2 balls torn into smaller pieces

Cheddar a handful of grated (optional, but really tasty)

Washed nettles about 100g leaves picked, use gloves when handling the nettles until cooked!

Oregano a sprinkle

1 — Roughly measure the water, yeast, sugar and olive oil in a jug. Whisk it all together and set aside for five minutes or so to let the yeast get to work. **2** — If you have a food mixer with a dough hook use this and weigh the flour and salt into the mixer bowl. Fix in the bowl and turn onto low speed whilst pouring the liquid in slowly. Once a dough has formed, turn up the speed and let it knead for around 5 minutes. **3** — If kneading by hand it's best to knead for about ten minutes, until the dough is soft, springy and when you poke it, it bounces back at you. Cover with a towel and set aside whilst you make the tomato sauce and gather your toppings. **4** — After an hour or so left in a warm place, the dough will have doubled in size. Preheat your oven to 200ºC / gas mark 6 and prepare some flat baking trays (as many as will fit in your oven), lining them with baking paper. **5** — Scrape the dough out onto a floured surface and split into 4 pieces. Roll each piece into a ball using your hands and then grab a rolling pin to roll them each into a flat pizza base shape. If a piece of dough is getting a bit too bouncy and not doing what you want, then leave it to rest for a few minutes before coming back to it. **6** — When you have 2 of your bases ready place them each on a tray and cover with a light spread of the tomato sauce, then the nettle leaves and the cheese. Top with a sprinkle of oregano and bake for 10 to 15 minutes each, until the cheese is golden and the dough is cooked through. Prepare your other 2 pizzas whilst the first batch is cooking and repeat.

★ *Kids, get out there picking those nettles! See our safety tips on page 10.*

Nettle pizza

Our school's Foraging Club once made pizzas with the rich pickings found on the school grounds. The children loved being in charge of designing their own pizza, and became wonderfully inventive in their creations, which included one nasturtium-stuffed calzone. My favourite was this nettle pizza, which is in effect a Margherita with a boost of fresh and free greens. Simple, but so delicious.

Chocolate bean chilli

This punchy, tasty veggie chilli is a million miles away from some of the watery versions I've tried before. This is a great dish to make with children as it's not too spicy, simple to cook and a chance to practise that chopping!

1 — Heat your oil in a large heavy bottomed saucepan over a medium heat and throw in the onions. **2** — Let them sweat for a few minutes before adding the garlic and spices. Cook for a few more minutes until fragrant. **3** — Add the carrots, parsnips and pearl barley, stirring for a few minutes before adding everything but the peppers. Add half a tomato tin of water and give everything a good stir before letting it bubble away for about half an hour. **4** — Test to see if the carrots are cooked through and if they are soft then add the peppers. Give everything another good stir then continue to let it simmer for at least a few more minutes to soften the peppers. **5** — Give it a taste, when it's rich, thick and delicious, it's ready to serve. **6** — Serve up with chopped coriander, rice, sweet potato fries, lime wedges and yoghurt for a full table load.

Serves 4 to 5

Start to finish 1 hr

—

Oil a glug

Onion 1 peeled and diced

Garlic 2 cloves squashed, peeled and diced

Cumin seeds 2 tsp

Chilli ½ tsp of powder or chilli flakes

Smoked paprika 2 tsp

Carrot 1 scrubbed and diced

Parsnip 1 scrubbed and diced

Pearl barley a handful

Beans 2 x 400g tins, drained and rinsed (kidney beans, cannellini beans or black beans work well)

Unsweetened cocoa 1 heaped tsp

Vinegar a splash of balsamic or red wine

Walnuts 100g (optional)

Chopped tomatoes 2 x 400g tins

Salt 2 tsp

Peppers 2 diced

Falafel scotch eggs

These scotch eggs are gorgeous-looking little snacks packed with goodness. There's no better veggie option for parties – and the kids love them because apparently they look like dinosaur eggs.

1 — Bring a medium saucepan of water to boil and line a small baking tray with baking paper, preheating your oven to 195°C / gas mark 6. **2** — Carefully add the eggs to the pan. Simmer for 6 minutes, then take them out – plunging them straight into cold water. **3** — While the eggs are cooling, start frying the onion. Add the garlic and spices once the onion has softened. The spices will start to smell great after a minute or so, then you can turn the heat off. Leave to cool a little whilst you shell the eggs. **4** — Tip the spiced onion mix into the food processor (or a bowl you can pop a stick blender into) and whiz to a paste. Add the chickpeas and coriander and pulse until it forms a very rough chopped mix. Remove from the food processor and stir through the flour, the one remaining egg and the tablespoon of breadcrumbs. **5** — Mix the remaining breadcrumbs with the sesame seeds. Take a handful of falafel mix and flatten it onto your palm, pop the egg on top and close your palm, wrapping the egg in mixture; squish it to seal as you go. Roll in your breadcrumbs mix and then put onto the prepared tray. **6** — Your eggs will need around 20 minutes in the oven, turning halfway.

Makes 8 eggs

Start to finish 1 hr

—

Eggs 9 (8 for boiling, 1 for the falafel mix)

Onions 1 peeled and roughly sliced

Garlic cloves 2 cloves squashed and peeled

Cumin 1 heaped tbsp

Coriander 1 tbsp

Chickpeas 400ml tin drained

Flour 5 tbsp

Breadcrumbs
1 heaped tbsp for falafel mix, 200g for coating

Flour 1 handful

Sesame seeds 3 tbsp

★ *What a great opportunity to teach your kids how to boil eggs! A vital life skill that will serve them throughout their teenage years, onto university and beyond.*

Everything in a jar!

Humble hummus

Hummus is such a perfect savoury snacking food, full of protein and healthy fats (bonus points if you dip fresh raw veg into it).

Serves 4 to 5 or a 450ml kilner jar

Start to finish 5 mins

—

Chickpeas 400g can

Tahini 1 big tbsp

Lemon half the juice and zest

Salt 1 tsp

Garlic 1 small clove

Pepper to taste

Extra virgin olive oil a glug

Cold water 2 tbsp to loosen

1 — Chuck everything in the food processor and blitz to a paste consistency, adding water if needed and to your taste. **2** — Taste to see if you think it needs more lemon or more salt. The secret to creamy smooth hummus is to let it blend for ages. Walk away from your blitzer and do something else (unless you have to hold it down like mine!). Come back a few minutes later and it'll be super smooth.

Five ways to take your hummus up a level: ★ *Add a handful of cooked diced beetroot. It becomes gloriously pink and so sweet. Perfect for a buffet table or potluck meal.* ★ *Use a tin of beans instead of chickpeas; aduki, borlotti and butter beans all work well.* ★ *Add a handful of roasted squash slices, for a sweeter flavour and a sunset-rich colour.* ★ *Sprinkle the top with toasted seeds for a bit of crunch.* ★ *Add a roasted red pepper from a jar and a pinch of paprika for a really tangy, smoky version.*

Cucumber tzatziki

This is an easy little dip that's great for a party table, or served up with roasted meats and burgers.

1 — Simply mix all your ingredients together and taste for seasoning.

Serves 450ml kilner jar

Start to finish 5 mins

—

Cucumber ½, julienned on a mandolin or chunky grated. (If the skin is tough, remove it.)

Greek style natural yoghurt 300ml (roughly)

Extra virgin olive oil 1 tbsp

Chilli flakes pinch (optional)

Salt and **pepper** to taste

Quick pickled chillies

Pickled chillies are great on top of rice, eggs, potatoes, soups and so much more. Perfectly sweet and sour, just a little bit spicy, so perfect for young ones. The vinegar mellows the hotness but still leaves it zingy! For the best flavour, go for organic chillies, and as you need quite a few, make sure you purchase them by weight from a proper veg shop or market rather than in the little packets of three from the supermarket.

Makes enough to fill a 450 ml kilner jar

Start to finish ½ hr

—

Water 125ml

Apple cider vinegar 200ml

Sugar 2 level tbsp

Salt 2 level tbsp

Fresh chillies 15 any colour, stalks chopped off

1 — Clean and sterilise your jar. Remove rubber seal, place the glass part in the oven and turn it on at 120°C / gas mark 1. Leave to warm up gently for around 20 minutes whilst you make the pickles. Make sure you use oven gloves when removing from the oven. **2** — Measure the water, vinegar, salt and sugar into a small pan. **3** — Stir over a low heat until the sugar and salt have both dissolved. **4** — Meanwhile, slice the chillies into rounds and place, seeds and all, into the hot jar. Wash your hands after working with chillies and don't touch your eyes! **5** — Once the liquid is piping hot and steaming, pour it over the chillies in the jar, filling the jar right to the top and submerging the chillies completely. Place the rubber seal back onto the lid and clip the top shut whilst still hot. **6** — Once the jar has cooled, give it a shake to ensure all the chillies are completely drowned. Do this every time you take from the jar. **7** — Give them a couple of days on the shelf for the flavours to soak in before getting stuck in.

★ *When you've finished a jar of gherkins, instead of throwing away the pickling liquid, heat it up to boiling point in a small pan whilst washing and sterilising the jar, fill the jar up with cucumber slices (or another veggie) and pour the hot liquid back in to the jar over the veggie.*

Razor sharp lemon curd

Makes 450ml kilner jar

Start to finish ½ hr

—

Lemons 4 zested and juiced

Sugar 200g

Butter 100g diced

Salt a tiny pinch

Eggs 3

This is a curd which is heavy on the lemon juice and easy on the sugar, making it deliciously sharp and really lemony. Eat it with loads of butter on real sourdough toast, stir into porridge or make a dessert by adding it to yoghurt or even whipped cream. I cook my curd directly in a heavy bottomed pan rather than in a bain-marie because it's less hassle, though beware, you must be very attentive whilst doing so or else you'll have lemon flavoured scrambled eggs on your hands!

1 — Zest and juice your lemons directly into a small, heavy bottomed saucepan. **2** — Add the sugar and diced butter. **3** — Dissolve over a low heat, stirring constantly with a whisk. **4** — Whisk the eggs in a jug with a fork. **5** — Take the pan off the heat and whisk to cool slightly. The sides of the pan shouldn't be too hot and it shouldn't be steaming, leave to cool if it is. **6** — Add the egg in a steady slow stream whilst whisking vigorously to make sure you don't scramble your eggs. **7** — When it's all incorporated, put back on the lowest heat and stir steadily with a wooden spoon or spatula, making sure you reach the bottom until the curd has become heavy and thick like custard. It will set properly as it cools. **8** — Take off the heat and pour into a clean jar. Once cooled keep in fridge, the curd will last for a couple of weeks.

★ *When zesting lemons, make sure you only grate off the yellow skin, not the white bitter pith; this is a great activity for children to do, along with the juicing.*

Really wild garlic pesto

Makes 450ml kilner jar, enough to stir through pasta for 4–5

Start to finish ¼ hr

—

Wild garlic leaves a large bunch freshly washed

Grated parmesan a handful of

Fresh basil a handful (optional)

Pine nuts a handful ideally toasted

Mild olive oil a glug

Salt a pinch

Lemon 1 zested and juiced

So tasty, so good for you, so easy, so adaptable, so fun to pick – this recipe has it all! It's also a fine example of flavour balancing sums! Sweet (garlic) + fatty (oil) + salty (parmesan) + acidic (lemon). In other sums, wild garlic pesto is also 1 million times tastier than the jarred supermarket stuff. You can do loads with the pesto, stir it through pasta, make pesto cheese on toast and, my favourite, whizz up a quick pesto omelette.

1 — Toast the pine nuts in a dry frying pan for a couple of minutes, shaking the pan to ensure they're toasted evenly. **2** — Pour into food processor when done to ensure they don't continue to toast in the hot pan. **3** — Add all the other ingredients to the blender, except the lemon juice. **4** — Blitz until the ingredients are chopped down and a purée is formed. If you can't fit all the garlic in in one go, put in half, blitz for a while and then add the rest. **5** — Taste and season further, adding the lemon juice bit by bit to freshen up the pesto. **6** — Pour into a jar and keep in your fridge for up to a week.

Super-speedy guacamole

Guacamole isn't just a superfast snack, it's also a superfood! Avocados are packed with omega-3 fatty acids and many essential vitamins and minerals. A perfect side for Mexican feasts, with nachos or sweet potato fries.

1 — Peel and de-stone the avocados, popping the insides into a mixing bowl big enough to give them a good mash up. **2** — Add the zest and juice of the lime and the pinch of salt. **3** — Add any of the prepared optional ingredients and give it all a good mix and crush with a fork, stopping when you have your desired consistency. **4** — Spoon into a small bowl for dipping and dunking, and top with a sprinkle of paprika or some chilli flakes.

Makes 450 ml jar, enough for 4–5 to dunk in

Start to finish 15 mins

—

Avocados 2 very ripe

Lime 1

Salt a pinch

—

OPTIONAL

Red chilli 1 minced or diced finely

Tomato 1 medium diced

Coriander half a pack, chopped finely

Onion 1 small white diced very finely

Paprika or chilli flakes to garnish

★ *If your avocados aren't ripe, don't try this recipe – it'll be disappointing. Pop them in a paper bag or in a bowl with some bananas overnight to ripen up – really, this works!*

Honey mustard dressing

Makes about half a 450ml kilner jar, enough to dress a big family salad

Start to finish 5 mins

—

Runny honey 1 tbsp

Wholegrain mustard 1 heaped tbsp

Light olive oil or sunflower oil 120ml

Cider vinegar 50ml

Salt and **pepper** a pinch of each

A good dressing has the power to bring a dull salad to life. This sweet and tangy variety has a bit of texture from the mustard seeds and adds va-va-voom to leaves as well as bringing extra flavour to steamed veg like broccoli.

1 — Stick all the ingredients in a jar and shake it up until the honey is dissolved and the oil and vinegar fully emulsified. Drizzle over your salad or hot steamed vegetables; if you're dressing leaves, toss them well to coat evenly. **2** — Keep it in the fridge and give it a shake each time you go to use it as it will settle back into its separate parts.

Golly gosh green sauce

Makes 450ml kilner jar, enough to dress up a couple of meals for 4 to 5

Start to finish ¼ hr

—

Capers 2 tbsp in vinegar or rinsed salted capers

Basil 30g

Dill 30g

Parsley 30g

Extra virgin olive oil 80ml

Cider vinegar 50ml

Salt and **pepper** a pinch

Spoon this tasty herb sauce onto grilled meat, fish or potatoes to give it flavour, colour and an extra zing! It really is enough to transform a plain meal into something special or to freshen up your leftovers. Feel free to mix and match the soft herbs you use, those odds and ends left over from recipes will last longer blitzed up, think of it as an alternative way to store and prolong your fresh herbs!

1 — Pop all the ingredients into the bowl of the food processor and pulse until everything is combined. **2** — Taste for seasoning adding a little more pepper, salt or vinegar to taste. **3** — Scrape into a kilner jar and store in the fridge for up to a week.

Nutty red pesto

A bit of a twist on a classic red pesto, it's so rich and moreish that I get a little bit addicted when there's a jar in my fridge! Tip: to shortcut the first two steps of this recipe, use a jar or can of roasted red peppers rather than grilling your own.

1 — Preheat your grill to its highest setting, pop the peppers on a baking tray, ideally packing them close together, chargrill and turn until the outside blackens and the insides are soft, sweet and smoky. **2** — Tip the peppers, which should now be soft and squelchy, into a clean bowl and cover quickly with cling-film. Let the peppers cool for half an hour or so. **3** — Once the peppers have cooled enough to handle, you should find that they slip easily out of their skins. Transfer them straight into the food processor, leaving skins and seeds behind but keeping any juice. **4** — Add the rest of the ingredients. Blitz to a smooth paste with any liquid from the peppers or sundried tomatoes. Taste and add some salt if you think it needs it. **5** — The paste should be loose and spreadable. If it's too thick add a little more olive oil or a drop of water. Store in the fridge for up to a week.

Makes enough to fill a 450 ml kilner jar

Start to finish 5–40 mins, depending on whether you grill your own peppers

—

Big red peppers 4

Jarred sundried tomatoes 5

Ground almonds 100g

Smoked paprika 1 tsp

Chilli flakes ½ tsp (optional)

Mild olive oil 100g

Grated parmesan cheese 50g

Lemon 1 zested

Salt and **pepper** to taste

Five ways to use this scrumptious red pesto: ★ For a perfect pasta bake: mix a good dollop with pasta, a handful of sweetcorn and torn up left over roast chicken, before spreading into a deep tray and covering with cheese. Bake for 20 minutes until golden and crunchy on top. ★ Spread a crusty roll with a tablespoon of pesto, some crunchy lettuce and some torn up mozzarella. ★ For a lazy lunch, mix with some rocket and a drained can of white beans and pile onto some toast. ★ Stir through steamed greens for side veggies with a twist. ★ Use as a dip, with raw celery, carrots and cucumber sticks.

Punchy puddings

Blackberry yoghurt cake

Makes 1 loaf cake tin, serving 8 to 10 people

Start to finish 1 hr

—

Plain flour 125g

Wholemeal spelt flour 125g

Golden caster sugar 160g

Baking powder 1½ tsp

Bicarbonate of soda ½ tsp

Salt 1 pinch

Sunflower oil or light olive oil 80g

Eggs 2

Natural yoghurt 250g

Vanilla bean paste 1 tsp

Lemons 2 zested

Fresh or frozen blackberries no need to defrost

Not only is this cake deliciously moist and wholesome it has the added bonus of taking about 10 minutes to throw together. If you have a blackberry bush nearby, that can include picking the fruit. It's my go-to cake and I use it to make the most of any fruit I lay my hands on; it never fails and even without fruit, it's still delicious.

1 — Heat oven to 180°C / gas mark 4, grease and line a loaf tin with baking paper. **2** — Combine all the dry ingredients in one bowl with a whisk. Combine all the wet ingredients in another bowl with the same whisk. Add the dry ingredients to the wet mix and mix with a spatula until it forms a batter, making sure you get right to the bottom. **3** — Stir through the blackberries and lemon zest very gently. **4** — Pour into the prepared tin and bake for 25–30 minutes. Check it's cooked through by sticking a knife into the middle, it should come out dry. **5** — Cool in the tin for ten minutes or so before turning out, sprinkling with icing sugar, topping with a couple of fresh blackberries and slicing up to devour.

Spiced milk pannacotta

A light and humble pannacotta recipe, modelled on the most comforting of winter bedtime soothers.

1 — Put the milk, cream and spices into a small heavy based saucepan. **2** — Warm the mix over a gentle low heat until it reaches a simmer. Turn off the heat and add the sugar. Leave for 10 to 15 minutes for the spices to infuse. **3** — Meanwhile soak the gelatine leaves in a little water until soft; this will take around 5 minutes. **4** — Squeeze the water out of the soft gelatine leaves and add them to the hot mix, stir to dissolve. **5** — Strain mix through a sieve into a jug. Pour into your moulds or jars, cover and pop in the fridge to set. This should only take a couple of hours but I find it easier to make the day before and leave overnight. **6** — To serve, either turn out onto a plate or eat straight from the jars.

Makes 4 to 5 jelly moulds or small jars

Start to finish ½ hr to make, overnight to set

—

Star anise 2

Cardamom pods 3 crushed

Cloves 5

Small cinnamon stick 1

Fresh ginger 1 child-sized thumb roughly chopped, no need to peel

Peppercorns 2

Milk 300ml

Double cream 200ml

Sugar 25g

Gelatine leaves 3

★ *If you are a vegetarian, switch the gelatine for an alternative and convert the quantity following packet instructions.*

Oranges and lemons flapjack

Serves 10 to 12

Start to finish 1 hr
plus cooling time

—

Orange 1 large

Lemon ½

Sultanas 100g

Unsalted butter 200g

Golden syrup 100g

Soft brown sugar 100g

Jumbo oats 300g

Plain flour 100g

Mixed toasted seeds
100g

Flapjacks are just the best way to stave off pangs for a sweet hit and are such a doddle to make. This version is a hit at the Marlborough School Cooking Club. What a delicious way to get little ones tucking into seeds and dried fruit.

1 — Preheat your oven to 160°C / gas mark 3 and grease and line a 20cm deep baking tray with baking paper. **2** — Zest all the citrus fruits into a large heat proof bowl and add the oats, flour and seeds. **3** — Juice the citrus fruits into a small saucepan, add the sultanas and heat gently until it's all piping hot. Then take off the heat and leave to one side, allowing the sultanas to plump up in the hot juice. **4** — Combine butter, syrup and sugar in another saucepan, large enough to allow good stirring, and warm through gently. Stir often with a wooden spoon until everything has melted and the sugar is no longer gritty. Then take off the heat. **5** — Combine the contents of both saucepans into the large bowl with the dry mix. Stir with a rubber spatula until there are no dry bits to be found lurking at the bottom. **6** — Tip into the prepared baking tray, spread evenly and bake for 15 minutes, or until golden brown. **7** — It's vital that you leave to cool in the tray before cutting the flapjacks; hard as it is to resist. I know!

★ *Pop your flapjack tray in the fridge overnight once its cool enough. They slice best when they're very cold.*

Five minute pomegranate and lemon curd bowl

Serves 4 to 5

Start to finish 5 mins

—

Plain yoghurt
(ideally Greek)
2 x 700ml tubs

Lemon curd 3 tbsp
home-made is even
more scrummy, see
ours on page 72

Pomegranate seeds
a large handful

Blueberries a scattering

Toasted oats or
chopped nuts (optional)

This pretty sweet treat is packed with superfood goodness and takes no more than a few minutes to prepare. Equally excellent served to the kids in a hastily prepared supper or as a casual but eye-popping desert for a lunch with friends.

1 — Swirl the yoghurt and lemon curd together, spoon into bowls. **2** — Top with pomegranate seeds and a scattering of blueberries. **3** — Add a sprinkling of toasted oats or chopped nuts if you're super hungry!

Foraged flower power fritters

These delicate sweet treats will delight discerning foodies and children alike. We've made these at school using dandelions and elderflowers drizzled with honey, and both versions were devoured in seconds.

1 — Whisk the flour with the egg and a drop or two of the milk until you have a smooth paste, then incorporate the rest of the milk to loosen. You should have a smooth batter with the consistency of custard. **2** — Heat the oil in a non-stick frying pan over a medium heat. When the oil is hot, test to see if it sizzles when a teeny bit of batter is dropped in. If it does it's ready to go. **3** — Dip a flower into the batter, let any excess drip off and then place in the frying pan. Cook for a couple of minutes before flipping over for a few more minutes. **4** — Place on a plate, drizzle with honey, a squeeze of lemon and eat immediately!

Serves 5

Start to finish ¼ hr

—

Flour 200g

Egg 1

Milk 200ml

Sunflower oil 1 glug

Foraged flowers a small bagful, dandelion, elderflower, courgette, squash, apple blossom and borage all work well

Runny honey and **lemon wedges** to serve

★ *Give flowers a good shake before dipping to get rid of any bugs that might be lurking!*

Sherbet blood orange plate

Packed with antioxidants and bursting with glorious colour and flavour, the blood orange is the perfect antidote to a grey January day. When we pile up our school fruit bowls with these rich red and pink quarters in the depths of winter, the children clamour for more. I'm not sure if it's the colour, the novelty or the tangy taste the kids love so much, but if you're looking for ways to give your children a blast of vitamin C and a taste of Sicilian sunshine, you can't beat blood oranges.

Serves 4 to 5

Start to finish ¼ hr

—

Blood oranges 4
or oranges of your choice

Ground cinnamon
approx. 1 tsp

Runny honey
1 heaped tsp

Vanilla ice cream
to serve (optional)

1 — Slice the tops and bottoms of the oranges using a small, serrated knife. This gives the fruit a flat bottom to sit on and reveals the juicy insides at the top. **2** — Peel the orange effectivly by sitting the orange's flat bottom on a board, cut downwards in a curved motion between the flesh and pith and orange skin. **3** — Slice thinly into rounds. Repeat with each orange. **4** — If this is too difficult, slice the orange vertically in half first and then place it on its flat centre and slice into thin half moons. **5** — Arrange the pieces on a pretty plate, drizzle with honey and dust with cinnamon. **6** — Leave for a couple of minutes to let the flavour of the cinnamon sink in before eating them all up. **7** — For an even more luxurious treat; try with vanilla ice cream.

Tropical rice pudding

Many adults are put off rice pudding, due to traumatic encounters with the lumpy, bland stodge they were served when they were young. Our head teacher, Mr Gambier, fell into this category, until I managed to persuade him to try this recipe. It is simply delicious.

1 — Scrape out vanilla seeds from the pod. **2** — Combine the rice, milk, coconut milk and the scraped out vanilla seeds and pod in a big heavy bottomed saucepan over a medium heat. **3** — When it starts to simmer, turn it down low and cook for 30–40 minutes until it's thick and the rice is soft. **4** — Keep an eye on the texture as it cooks. If it starts to dry out add more milk or water. **5** — Take the pudding off the hob and stir through the apricots and desiccated coconut if using. **6** — Add your chosen sweetener to taste. You should only need about a tablespoon's worth as the apricots will do half the job for you. **7** — Serve in bowls, sprinkle with mango, pomegranate seeds and flaked coconut.

Serves 4 to 5

Start to finish ¾ hr

—

Pudding rice 200g

Milk 500g

Coconut milk 400g

Vanilla pod 1

Un-sulphured apricots a handful, chopped

Desiccated coconut a small handful (optional)

Sugar, honey or other sweetener to taste

Mango, flaked coconut and **pomegranate seeds** to decorate the top (optional)

★ *Test your kids' tasting abilities and let them add the sweetener at the end, getting them to stop as soon as it tastes sweet.*

Brilliant banana-pops

Makes 8 lollies

Start to finish ½ hr plus a couple of hours in the freezer

—

Bananas 4

Thick Greek yoghurt 100ml

Runny honey 1 tsp

—

TOPPING IDEAS

Go wild and experiment, here are some starting points...

Strawberries a few fresh thinly diced

Melted chocolate

Unsweetened desiccated coconut

Hundreds and thousands for a retro fab vibe

Chopped toasted nuts

Freeze dried strawberries or raspberries, whizzed up to make a powder

These are a cheap and tasty alternative to shop bought ice lollies and ice creams, perfectly sized for a little snack or summer pudding. Kids absolutely adore making these, though you may find they want to eat them all the day they are frozen!

1 — To begin, slice the bananas in half right through the middle and peel each side. **2** — Stick a lolly stick into the centre of the cut end of the banana half, this gives you your basic banana-pop. You can freeze them at this point and they are completely delicious. Proceed for more fun though. **3** — Mix the honey and yoghurt in a small bowl and line a tray with greaseproof paper. **4** — Using a teaspoon, coat each lolly carefully with the yogurt mix. **5** — Sprinkle or dip into your chosen toppings, pick and mix until your heart's content. **6** — Freeze for a couple of hours at least before eating. They will last in a sealed tub in the freezer for about a month.

Apple and elderberry crumble

We don't serve pudding much at school, most days we have a table in our lunch hall laden with all different types of fruit. But when we do, it's most often a version of this crumble and we have to choose the day carefully as it's been known to whip our pupils into a near frenzied state, clamouring and falling over each other for seconds.

1 — Preheat oven to 180°C / gas mark 4. Place your apples in an appropriately sized deep heavy baking dish, you want a bit of room left for the topping in there. **2** — Sprinkle the berries over the apples and pour in the juice. **3** — In a large mixing bowl (or a free standing mixer with the paddle attachment) combine all the other ingredients and rub in with your fingertips (or turn on the mixer, making sure it's on low speed so the ingredients don't fly out). The mixture will start to look like breadcrumbs with the occasional clump, don't worry if all the butter doesn't disappear into the mix. **4** — Sprinkle your topping over your base, press down if you like a compact crumble. **5** — Bake for about 30 mins until golden and the apple is soft when prodded with a knife. Serve with real custard, double cream or crème fraîche.

Serves 4 to 5 with leftovers

Start to finish 1 hr

—

Sweet apples 600g roughly chopped, no need to peel

Elderberries 50g (blackcurrants work well if it's the wrong time of year)

Apple juice a splash

Plain flour 100g

Spelt flour 100g

Jumbo oats 100g

Golden caster sugar 75g

Ground cinnamon 1 heaped tsp

Unsalted butter 150g chopped into cubes

Salt 1 pinch

Give these other fillings a try: ★ 600g chopped rhubarb, a handful of chopped dates and some chopped stem ginger in syrup. ★ 600g chopped pears, a couple of handfuls of blackberries – replace 30g of flour with cocoa in the topping. ★ 600g chopped apples, a large pinch of allspice and a handful of sultanas. ★ a tray full of frozen berries with a big chopped Bramley apple and a sprinkling of flaked almonds on top.

★ Why not make the most of all that rubbing in and double the topping quantities, freezing a batch for an even easier weeknight pud one night soon.

Sides, drinks and other bits!

Smoked mackerel pâté stars

Serves 4 to 5

Start to finish ½ hr

—

STARS

Good quality loaf of bread or baguette

Salt a pinch

Pepper a pinch

Chilli flakes a pinch

Olive oil 100ml

—

PÂTÉ

Smoked mackerel fillets 3–4 removed from skin and checked for bones

Cream cheese 150g full fat please!

Crème fraîche or yoghurt 100g

Lemon 1 juice and zest

Dill a small handful of chopped – leave some to sprinkle on top of the finished stars

Cucumber slices to garnish (optional)

Perfect for lunching in the garden with friends and family, this is a light, simple and wonderfully moreish dish that everyone will love. If you can, go for locally smoked mackerel; there's nothing better.

For the stars

1 — Preheat your oven to 180°C / gas mark 4. **2** — Pop a cooling rack onto a flat tray. Baking the stars on this means they don't need flipping and excess oil can drip off. **3** — Slice the bread as thinly as possible without it crumbling and using a star shaped cutter (or another shape) press stars out from your slices. **4** — Season the oil with the salt, chilli and pepper. **5** — Take your bread shapes and brush them all over with the seasoned olive oil using a pastry brush, place on rack, fitting them in snugly if need be, but not overlapping. **6** — Bake in the oven until golden, around 10 minutes, leave to cool before moving.

For the pâté

1 — While stars are in the oven, it's time to tackle the pâté. First, place half the mackerel, the cream cheese and crème fraîche in a food processor and blitz until smooth before removing to a bowl. **2** — Throw in the lemon zest, chopped dill and a squeeze of lemon juice, then fold in the rest of the mackerel, broken up. **3** — Taste and add more pepper or lemon juice accordingly. **4** — To serve; spread a spoonful of pâté onto a star and top with chopped dill and sliced cucumber.

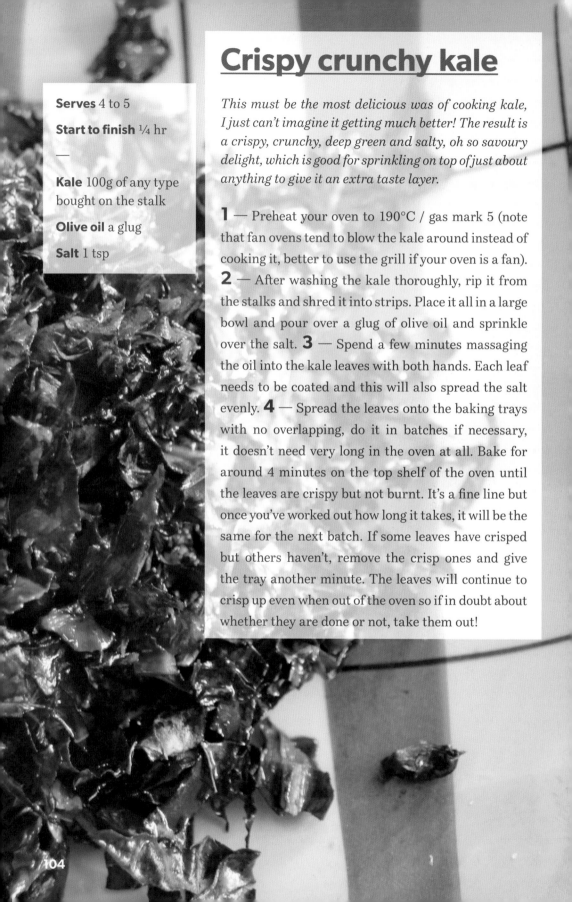

Crispy crunchy kale

Serves 4 to 5

Start to finish ¼ hr

—

Kale 100g of any type bought on the stalk

Olive oil a glug

Salt 1 tsp

This must be the most delicious was of cooking kale, I just can't imagine it getting much better! The result is a crispy, crunchy, deep green and salty, oh so savoury delight, which is good for sprinkling on top of just about anything to give it an extra taste layer.

1 — Preheat your oven to 190°C / gas mark 5 (note that fan ovens tend to blow the kale around instead of cooking it, better to use the grill if your oven is a fan). **2** — After washing the kale thoroughly, rip it from the stalks and shred it into strips. Place it all in a large bowl and pour over a glug of olive oil and sprinkle over the salt. **3** — Spend a few minutes massaging the oil into the kale leaves with both hands. Each leaf needs to be coated and this will also spread the salt evenly. **4** — Spread the leaves onto the baking trays with no overlapping, do it in batches if necessary, it doesn't need very long in the oven at all. Bake for around 4 minutes on the top shelf of the oven until the leaves are crispy but not burnt. It's a fine line but once you've worked out how long it takes, it will be the same for the next batch. If some leaves have crisped but others haven't, remove the crisp ones and give the tray another minute. The leaves will continue to crisp up even when out of the oven so if in doubt about whether they are done or not, take them out!

Buttery beetroot

Serves 4 to 5

Start to finish 20 mins

—

Beetroots 3–4 (500g)

Salted butter
2 tbsp (50g)

Balsamic vinegar

Allspice a pinch

1 — Peel and grate your beetroot, or simply chuck it in the food processor, with the grater attachment on, to save yourself a bit of time. **2** — Place all the ingredients in a saucepan, cover and cook on a medium heat for around 10 minutes or until the beetroot is soft, butter has melted in and the balsamic has reduced. The mix will be glossy and shouldn't have much excess liquid. **3** — Serve straight away or put aside ready to reheat when needed.

Celeriac and potato gratin

I fully embrace and savour meals with a good dose of cream in once in a while, and this bake definitely falls in to that category. Serve with something fuss free (like sausages) that you can just stick in the already warmed up oven whilst concentrating on your bake. To top off a completely alpine-mountain-worthy feast, serve with our buttered beetroot on page 105.

1 — Preheat oven to 160°C / gas mark 3. **2** — Combine cream, milk, garlic and spices in heavy-based saucepan with lid. **3** — Peel and slice both potatoes and celeriac into ½ cm thick slices. Add the slices to the pan. **4** — Put the pan on a medium heat, cover and wait until it begins to simmer. Turn it down to minimum heat and let it simmer very gently for 10 minutes. The veg should start to soften. **5** — Scoop the celeriac and potato out with a fish slice, place into the ovenproof dish, spread evenly with the slices roughly stacking side by side and on top of one another. Remove the star anise and bay. **6** — Pour over the remaining cream in the pan and shake ovenproof dish to even it all out, cover the top with breadcrumbs. **7** — Bake for 30–40 minutes until you can poke down through easily with a knife. **8** — Let it sit for 10 minutes before serving as it will be molten hot.

Serves 5 to 6

Start to finish 1 hr

—

Double cream 300ml

Milk 200ml

Star anise 2

Bay leaves 2

Garlic clove 1 fat peeled and thinly sliced

Celeriac 1 medium (roughly 1kg in weight, unpeeled)

Medium potatoes 2 (roughly 300g in weight), scrubbed, no need to peel

Salt and **pepper** a big pinch of each

Fresh breadcrumbs a handful

Root veg rosties

These are a super way to use up rogue root vegetables lurking at the bottom of the fridge – serve as a snack or starter with crème fraîche to dip into, or make a meal of it by serving with some salad and poached eggs. We've used beetroot for our recipe below, but feel free to swap in around 200g of carrots, celeriac, swede, parsnip or any other root vegetable.

Makes 10 small rosties

Start to finish ½ hr

—

Large beetroot 1 grated on a mandolin or sliced into matchsticks

Medium potato 1 grated on a mandolin or sliced into matchsticks

Small onion 1 sliced thinly

Gram flour 3 heaped tbsp

Eggs 2

Lime 1 zest and juice

Salt and **pepper**

Dill 1 tbsp chopped

Sunflower oil a glug

Crème fraîche (optional)

1 — Mix all the ingredients except the crème fraîche together in a large bowl, set aside until ready to cook. **2** — Heat a large, non-stick frying pan and add a glug of oil. Wait until it's good and hot. Test by dropping a little mix into the pan – if it sizzles, it's ready. **3** — Drop about a tablespoon of mixture into the pan at a time, giving each dollop a little room around it to enable a flip. **4** — Let them fry for a couple of minutes before slipping a fish slice underneath each one and flipping it over, pressing down its top to flatten it out. **5** — After they've had a couple of minutes on each side, they will be ready to go, serve immediately or keep warm on a plate in a low oven. **6** — Serve dipped in crème fraîche.

★ *Adding around two tablespoons worth of chopped smoked salmon trimmings to this mix is a great variation.*

A most colourful coleslaw

'Slaw like you've never tasted before. Never again will you limit yourself to carrot and cabbage coleslaw; it can be so much more! Big batches will last a few days and are perfect for packed lunches or with quick dinners of jacket spuds, halloumi or burgers.

1 — First up, it's a big chopping job. This is a great exercise in chopping and preparing raw vegetables for the kids, so why not get them to help prepare all your ingredients? The idea is to get all of your vegetables sliced as thinly as possible, or into matchsticks. Use a mandolin if you are confident, or a big sharp knife and some precision. **2** — Now simply combine all your carefully chopped veg in a large bowl, add the yoghurt, mayonnaise, juice, zest and seeds and mix well. **3** — If it's a little dry add a more yoghurt or mayonnaise... or both!

Serves 4 to 5

Start to finish ¼ hr

—

Carrot 1

Small beetroot 1

White or **red cabbage** quarter or half a bunch of spring greens

Small kohlrabi or celeriac peeled

Onion a half

Crunchy apple 1

Natural full fat yoghurt 2 tbsp

Mayonnaise 2 tbsp

Lemon 1 zest and juice

Mixed seeds 2 tbsp (optional)

Cheesy polenta triangles

For those times when you're sick of endless potatoes and pasta, polenta is perfect. It's a northern Italian speciality, made from corn, which you can buy in two ways: dried or in a ready-made set block. We use dried in this recipe, which is extremely cheap and lasts forever. These triangles are best served with something wet, I like them with guacamole, or, if I'm feeling lazy, with baked beans or sweet chilli sauce.

Serves 4 to 5

Start to finish 1 ½ hrs

—

Olive oil for drizzling and greasing tray

Water 1200ml

Bouillon powder 1 tbsp

Polenta 250g

Salt and **pepper** a big pinch

Dried oregano a heaped tsp

Chilli flakes 1 tsp

Strong cheddar 100g grated

1 — Oil a deep oven tray 30cm x 20cm. Heat the water in a large heavy-based pan. Add the bouillon powder. **2** — When the water is simmering add the polenta, the salt, oregano and chilli flakes. **3** — Stir well and continuously, watch out that it's not boiling too fast as it can splat and burn, keep it gentle, add more water if it becomes stiff. You should mix until you have a smooth paste then keep stirring over heat for a few minutes to cook the polenta through. **4** — Remove from the heat and add the cheese, stirring well. Taste for seasoning, being very careful to cool your spoon as it will be lava hot! **5** — Pour into your oiled tray and spread until flat with a spatula, (rub the spatula on the bottom of the oiled tray first to grease it for easy spreading). **6** — Allow to cool, this will take a couple of hours. Why not leave overnight in the fridge for the next day? **7** — When ready to bake, preheat the oven to 200ºC / gas mark 6 and line or grease a flat baking tray. Place the set polenta block onto a chopping board and chop into desired shapes. Arrange the shapes on the tray, giving them as much room as possible. Drizzle with olive oil and bake for 10 minutes before flipping over with a burger flipper and bake for 10 minutes more. Serve immediately!

★ *The set polenta will keep in the fridge for a couple of days very well, so it's a perfect make ahead, or just keep some chopped at the ready for the next time hunger strikes!*

Chorizo patatas bravas

This is a yummy potato dish, whipped up after a request from some of our Year 4 girls, who were dreaming of tapas from their summer holidays. We sometimes swap the chorizo for a tin of drained chickpeas to add a bit of protein to a veggie version.

Serves 4 to 5 as a side

Start to finish ¾ hr

—

Potatoes around 1kg all-rounder, washed and scrubbed

Smoked paprika 1 heaped tbsp

Olive oil a glug

Chorizo 200g of cooking chorizo, crumbled or 200g cured chorizo sausage chopped

Sea salt 1 tsp

Lemon 1 zested

Flat leaf parsley 1 tbsp to finish

1 — Preheat your oven to 180°C / gas mark 4. **2** — Roughly cube your potatoes into 2cm dice, (no need to peel) and throw into a deep roasting tray along with the olive oil, paprika, chorizo and salt. **3** — Give it all a good mix with your hands, getting the paprika really well mixed in. **4** — Bake in the oven for around 30 minutes, moving them around midway. **5** — When done they should be soft, a bit smashed up but with some crunchy edges! **6** — Serve immediately, with chopped parsley stirred in and the zest of a lemon on top.

★ *This could be the perfect accompaniment to a mid summer roast chicken, when it's a little bit too hot to be faffing around making gravy. Stuff the chicken with lots of lemon wedges and serve with aioli and green garden salad (see page 118).*

Lazy sweet potato chips

These baked fries are as sweet, salty and moreish as the deep fried version you get at fancy burger bars. An extremely sociable snack or starter, pile them high, line up the dips and get dunking!

1 — Begin by preheating your oven to 200°C / gas mark 6 and dig out a couple of large flat trays. Chop the sweet potato (no need to peel) into 1cm wide, tall sticks with a large sharp knife, try to keep them all roughly the same diameter. **2** — Pop the sweet potato sticks in a large bowl or a clean sink and cover with cold water. Give them a good wriggle around under water and then drain off in a colander after a minute or so. Throw the chips onto a clean tea towel and roughly dry. Dry the bowl too. **3** — Place the dry chips back in the bowl and add the oil and cornmeal. Toss it all around until the fries are well coated. **4** — Spread the fries out onto flat trays, ensuring that they are not touching each other. I line them up in a slightly militantly neat way! Sprinkle with salt and pepper and bake for around 20 minutes until they're golden and crisp

Serves 4 to 5

Start to finish ½ hr

—

Large washed sweet potatoes with skins 4

Sunflower oil
a large glug

Cornmeal or fine
polenta, a small handful

Salt and **pepper**
to season

★ *For a nutty flavour boost, add some sesame seeds to the bowl when coating and then sprinkle with smoked paprika when they are laid out on the tray.*

Serves 4 to 5

Start to finish ¼ hr

—

Mixed leaf salad or
fresh baby spinach 100g
(organic if possible,
lots of farm shops sell
this now); alternatively
buy a nice big lettuce of
your choice, wash and
shred the leaves as your
starting point

Mixed fresh soft herbs
a handful (around 30g) –
dill, basil, mint, parsley
or coriander, roughly
chopped

—

OPTIONAL ADDITIONS

Marigold head washed
and petals picked for use

Borage flowers a
handful washed

Nasturtium flowers
and **leaves** washed and
leaves chopped

Chive flowers washed
and petals picked for use

**Young beetroot and
chard leaves** cut and
washed

Cherry tomatoes a
handful washed and
quartered

Show stealing garden salad

*Next time you're throwing together a little leafy number,
nip outside and see if there's anything you can find in the
wild to give it a bit of a lift and add a bit more colour
and freshness.*

1 — Make sure everything is washed, dried and
prepared as instructed. **2** — Combine in a big wide
salad bowl and drizzle with honey mustard dressing
(page 76) or your chosen dressing. **3** — Give everything
a good mix or leave this to be done at the table before
serving.

★ *Colourful rainbow chard is a great thing to grow if you've
got a little patch in the garden, you can sow seeds directly
into the ground in spring and either wait for the leaves to
grow large for cooking or pick the young leaves for salad
like we've done here. Don't worry, after picking, the leaves
will regrow and your chard will keep on giving!*

Popeye's cheese straws

These cheese straws are fantastic for shoehorning some greens into a party food table and you can guarantee they'll be the first thing to be snapped up.

1 — Line a large, flat baking tray with baking paper and preheat the oven to 190°C / gas mark 5. **2** — Flour a clean work surface and begin to roll out the chilled pastry. You want a large rectangle, about the thickness of a pound coin. Keep the pastry floured underneath, moving it 90 degrees every now and then to work it in each direction and stop it sticking. Turn the shape so that a long edge is at the front facing you. Cover the bottom half of the rectangle with the spinach, then cover the spinach with cheese leaving a handful to sprinkle on the top. **3** — Wet your fingers or a pastry brush and run along the edges of the dough before folding the top half down over the filled bottom. Match up the edges and press it to close, folding in any wobbly edges you're not happy with. Roll it over again with the rolling pin in each direction to press the two sides together and flatten in any folded edges. Transfer your rectangle onto the baking sheet and with a pizza wheel, slice into long thin slices. Leave them sitting next to each other. **4** — Sprinkle with the remaining cheese and grind over some pepper if you wish. **5** — Bake for 20–25 minutes until golden brown. Lift a couple up to check the pastry is cooked through and you don't have any soggy bottoms! **6** — Leave to cool on the tray, re-slicing with the pizza wheel after about half an hour when they are ready to be moved.

Makes 15 short, or 8 long, straws

Start to finish ¾ hr

—

Puff pastry 1 x 400g batch (page 135)

Spinach 50g fresh leaves

Mature cheddar cheese 250g grated

Pepper to taste

Fruity crisps

Serves 4 to 5 and
some to keep for later

Start to finish 5–10
minutes for chopping,
and up to 4 hours in
the dehydrator or
¾ hr in the oven

—

Apples 3

Pears 3

Cinnamon
a couple of pinches

I got my hands on a dehydrator for £3 at a car boot sale and discovered that it's perfect for making these tasty fruity crisps. The kids love making them, and it's the perfect activity for helping them practise precise chopping skills.

1 — Finely slice 3 apples and 3 pears into rings. Be sure to keep the star-shaped core as it's so pretty. If this is a little hard for little people, cut them in half first so they have a flat bottom so chop on.

Dehydrator

If you are using a dehydrator, turn it to a medium setting, lay each slice on the dehydrator shelves, sprinkle with the cinnamon and stack your shelves on the dehydrator. Leave for 4 hours, switching the shelves from bottom to top around halfway through.

Or oven bake

To ovenbake, preheat oven to 110°C / gas mark 1 and bake on a lined tray sprinkled with cinnamon for 45 minutes until dry, they will crisp up on cooling.

★ *Once you've learnt the technique with apples and pears, move on to bananas and mangos, they're delicious!*

Overnight tray bake loaf

This large, soft tray loaf is a great start if you're keen to develop your own home baking routine. Finish with rosemary, sea salt and olive oil if you fancy chopping it up into focaccia-style chunks. As with all slow doughs, the timings can be affected a lot by the environment in which you're baking, so if you don't achieve perfection first time round just adjust your approach a little and try again. This makes a large loaf perfect for a crowd; if you're feeding fewer, just halve the ingredients.

1 — Using a free standing mixer, insert the dough hook and combine the two flours with the salt and yeast, start the mixer on the lowest speed. Add the water in a steady stream, stopping short of 650ml if it becomes very sticky. **2** — Increase the speed of the mixer and knead for around five minutes until you get a fairly loose dough that has come away from the sides of the bowl. It should be smooth, stretchy and bounce back when prodded. **3** — Cover, leaving in a warm place for around an hour until doubled in size. **4** — Line your tray with baking paper. Bring the dough back out onto your clean, floured work surface. Flatten and stretch the dough into the shape of your tray, using a rolling pin if necessary. **5** — Place into the tray covering with a tea towel and put your tray into the fridge, on its own shelf with a little space to grow. **6** — Leave the dough overnight in the fridge until you are ready to bake. **7** — Bring the tray out of the fridge and wait half an hour or so for the dough to come a little closer to room temperature, while you heat the oven to 180°C / gas mark 4. **8** — Prod deep holes all over the dough with your fore finger and then bake on the middle shelf of the oven for around 30 minutes, until it is golden, still soft but cooked all the way through.

Serves 1 large loaf

Start to finish 1 ½ hrs plus overnight proving

—

Strong white flour 330g

Strong wholemeal flour 630g

Fresh yeast 15g crumbled or a 7g sachet of dried yeast

Salt 15g

Cold water 650ml

Grilled chewy flatbreads

Makes 8 flatbreads

Start to finish ½ hr plus 2 hrs proving

—

Fast action dried yeast 7g sachet or 15g fresh yeast

Olive oil 1 glug

Sugar 1 tsp

Salt 1 tsp

Plain flour 350g plus more for rolling out

These are great for serving with stews, soups or anything dunkable. You could also rip them open and make sandwiches or cook them on the BBQ. Flatbreads take just minutes to cook and are great made a little thinner so you can fold them around a kebab or burger.

1 — Combine the yeast, oil, salt and sugar in a jug with 200ml warm water, whisk to dissolve and set aside for 10 minutes until the mix begins to froth. **2** — Weigh the flour into a large bowl and add the liquid, bringing together with your hands to make a dough. Knead for 5 to 10 minutes until the dough is stretchy and springy. Cover and prove for a couple of hours until it has doubled in size. **3** — Squidge the dough down, knocking it back; then leave covered again for another half an hour. **4** — Split the dough into 8 pieces, roll each one into a ball on a floured worktop and then roll flat with a rolling pin or simply flatten with your hands. **5** — Heat a grill pan for 5 minutes or so until screeching hot and then throw your flatbread on, turning after about a minute. Give it another half a minute on the other side. It should be cooked through and charred on the outside. If using a BBQ the same method is required, a minute or so on each side should do the trick! **6** — Eat them warm and fresh.

★ *Got any flatbreads left over? Rip them into little pieces and toss in a bowl with olive oil or even better garlic oil. Fry them up in a pan and you will have perfect crispy croutons for soup or a salad.*

Speedy soda bread

Makes 2 small loaves, enough to feed 6 to 8

Start to finish ¾ hr

—

Plain flour 600g or a mix of plain, wholemeal or spelt

Baking powder 2 ½ tsp

Salt 1 tsp

Bicarbonate of soda 1 tsp

Natural yoghurt 100–200ml made up to 500ml with water

Not much tops the simple deliciousness of freshly made bread with butter. Soda bread is quick to make and is the perfect match for warming soups and stews.

1 — Preheat oven to 200°C / gas mark 6 and line a flat rectangular baking tray with baking paper. **2** — Whisk the dry ingredients in a large bowl. **3** — Whisk the wet ingredients in a separate jug, then pour into the dry mix.Stir to bring the mix together with a rubber spatula, as soon as it's dough-like stop mixing as you don't want to overwork it. Work in any extra ingredients at this point. **4** — Divide your dough into two, knead each piece briefly into a round and put onto tray. **5** — Flatten each round until it's about 2cm thick and flour the surface liberally. **6** — Use a knife or a metal dough cutter to slice a cross shape right down into each round, making the bread easy to tear apart when baked. **7** — Bake for 20–25 mins until loaves are golden and sound hollow when tapped from underneath.

Why not try adding: ★ *a handful of grated mature cheddar cheese and toasted seeds.* ★ *100g diced blue cheese and a handful of toasted walnuts.* ★ *A handful of dried fruit, plumped in hot water. This variation is great served with cheese.*

★ *This loaf is best eaten fresh on its day of baking or as toast the next day. If any lasts longer than this, blitz it up in the food processor to breadcrumbs and stick them in the freezer. Use to top oven bakes, make treacle tarts or thicken soups!*

Serves 2 to 3

Start to finish ½ hr

—

Squash or sweet potato 220g cubed and boiled/steamed until soft

Ice a handful

Whole milk 1 pint

Coconut milk 400ml

Cinnamon 1 tsp

Nutmeg half grated

Banana 1

Maple syrup 1 tbsp

Squash smoothie

You might want to try giving this unusual but delicious smoothie to the children in a 'blind tasting' to see if they can guess what's in it. That way, they'll love it before they judge it! The maple syrup gives it the sweet lift which elevates this creamy drink to heavenly heights. Lush.

1 — Boil or steam the squash or sweet potato until soft, leave to cool. **2** — Whiz the cooled veg with the rest of the ingredients in a smoothie maker or liquidizer. **3** — Taste to check for sweetness, adding a little more maple syrup if desired, then slurp it up immediately!

Banana milkshake

This recipe is great for little kids to make with you as nothing needs chopping or measuring exactly. It's all peel, pinch, scoop and pour.

1 — Whiz it all up in a smoothie maker (or in a bowl with a stick blender) and pour into glasses and slurp it up.

Optional extras:
- ★ *Add 2 tbsp of peanut butter or handful of almonds for a nutty flavour and extra protein.*
- ★ *Add 1 tsp of cocoa to make it super chocolatey.*
- ★ *Make using nut, oat or coconut milk for a lighter version.*
- ★ *Add a handful of frozen berries for a fruity twist.*

Serves 2 to 3

Start to finish 10 mins

—

Bananas 2

Ice a handful

Natural yoghurt 3 tbsp

Cinnamon a pinch (plus sprinkle for the top)

Whole milk 250ml

Party pink lemonade

Serves 4 to 5

Start to finish ½ hr
plus overnight soak

—

Lemons 6 large

Golden caster sugar
125g

Water 1.5 litres

Beetroot 20g peeled
sliced raw, this is a tiny
amount so choose a
baby one and grate the
rest into a salad or
pasta sauce

*Summery and sharp, this drink is perfect for parties,
tumbled with fizzy water (read prosecco for the adults!)
and plenty of ice. Unleash your inner crazy scientist and
discover beetroot's incredible power to dye everything
pink!*

1 — Pare your lemons using a peeler, go around 3
of your lemons, taking off the yellow skin bit by bit,
bringing with you as little of the white pith underneath
as possible. Place the lemon peel into a large heatproof
bowl, add the sugar and the juice of all your lemons
(which should be around 200ml). **2** — Meanwhile,
boil a full kettle. **3** — Add 1.5 litres of boiling water
to the bowl and mix well to dissolve sugar. **4** —
Add the beetroot slices and watch it change colour!
5 — Cover the bowl and leave somewhere cool
overnight. **6** — In the morning, sieve the mix into a jug
and pour into recycled clean bottles. Store in the fridge
for up to a week. Shake before drinking.

★ *For a rhubarb twist, dice three stalks of rhubarb and heat
them gently with a splash of water until they've softened
and you are able to mash them with a wooden spoon.
Add to the mix before leaving overnight.*

Wobbly white sauce

A smooth, well-seasoned, flavoursome white sauce is a kitchen essential, the base for a lot of comforting favourites: macaroni cheese, lasagne and fish pie.

1 — Melt the butter in a small non-stick pan, whisking the flour in once it's started to melt. It should form a thick paste, so let it cook for a minute or so whilst whisking to ensure it is lump free. **2** — Add the bay leaf and then the milk, one glug at a time (a child-sized assistant could be helpful here) whilst whisking, whisking and whisking some more. **3** — As soon as the paste becomes smooth and sauce-like, you are safe to switch to a wooden spoon. Keep stirring, making sure you reach the bottom and all inside edges of the pan so it doesn't stick. **4** — Stir until it bubbles, then let it bubble for a couple of minutes more; this will get rid of the floury taste. **5** — Turn off the hob, let it cool for a couple of minutes then stir in the grated nutmeg. **6** — If you're not using your sauce straight away, you can stop it forming a skin by covering the surface of the sauce directly with cling film. If you're using it pretty soon, just cover the pan with its lid to keep it warm.

Makes 1 batch

Start to finish ¼ hr

—

Butter 50g

Plain flour 50g

Milk 568ml / 1 pint

Bay leaf 1

Nutmeg ½, grated on microplane

Salt and **pepper** to season

Cheat's puff pastry

Makes 2 batches weighing around 400g each, use a batch now and stick the rest in the freezer for next time

Start to finish ¼ hr

—

Plain flour 250g

Wholemeal flour 100g (optional, feel free to replace with another 100g of plain flour)

Salted butter 250g frozen

Cold water 150–200ml to bind

This is an awesomely easy pastry recipe that I've been using for years. It is failsafe and perfect for cheese straws, pasties, homity pies, deep-filled quiches and mince pies. So even if you tend to buy ready-made pastry from the supermarket, try this first. Honestly it's easy to make and it works.

1 — Weigh the flour into a large bowl. **2** — Unwrap the frozen butter and wrap in foil to stop it melting in your hands whilst you grate it. **3** — Grate it into the flour as quickly as possible. **4** — Mix briefly with your hands to coat the butter in the flour. **5** — Using a spatula, start mixing while adding water a few drops at a time. Keep mixing until a dough-like mass beings to form, then get your hands in there and bring it all together until smooth. **6** — Wrap the dough in cling film and chill until needed, giving it at least 30 minutes.

Big fat tomato sauce

Makes enough to stir through pasta for 4 to 5 with enough left over to freeze

Start to finish 1 hr

—

Aubergine 1

Red peppers 2

Onion 1 chopped

Garlic cloves 2 roughly chopped

Carrots 3 scrubbed and diced

Leek 1 scrubbed and roughly chopped

Celery 2 sticks scrubbed and roughly chopped

Good quality chopped tomatoes 2 x 400g tins

Fresh spinach a couple of handfuls or kale

Salt and **pepper** to taste

This sauce is a fundamental recipe in our school kitchen and we use it in many forms and guises. Aubergine can be a tricky sell, so this is a great way of sneaking it in. It's great for batch freezing or using as a base for pasta, pizzas, soup or stews.

1 — Set your oven to as high as it will go, stab your aubergine and peppers a couple of times and pop on a tray. Cook in the oven for 15 minutes until the skins are blackened and the veg has a deflated look about it. Tip into a heatproof bowl and cover with cling film. Set aside until cool enough to handle. **2** — Meanwhile, start your sauce by sloshing a glug of olive oil in a large heavy bottomed pan and then adding your onions, carrots, leeks, celery and garlic cloves. Sauté your veg mix on a low temperature until it softens and starts to take a bit of colour. **3** — Throw in your tomatoes and a cup of water and turn up the heat. Let it come to the boil then stick a lid on and simmer until the veg is soft, around 20 minutes. **4** — At this point, your baked veg should be cool enough to handle. Slip the peppers out of their skins and into the sauce. Rip off the aubergine skins and slide the soggy inners into the sauce. Add the spinach or kale and let it cook for a few minutes. **5** — Get your hand held stick blender ready to go. Take the sauce of the heat and blend until the sauce is smooth. **6** — Taste and add a little salt and pepper if you like. Use straight away or let your sauce cool before freezing.

★ *This is a really flexible recipe, don't be put off making it if you don't have some of the vegetables, use it in a way that works for you and your kitchen.*

Thank you, thank you, thank you...

For the past two years Ruth Littlejohns-Sames and I have been beavering away in between our day jobs to publish Feed. There have been highs when we managed to cook and shoot seven dishes in five hours!
A low when the panna cotta cat didn't quite make the cut due to it totally collapsing. We never gave up; we knew that we had to share with you what we were cooking up in the Marlborough School Kitchen.

Ruth has not only managed the project but taken all the photographs, run illustration workshops, pitched for funding, organised and styled shoots and even written a few words while juggling mummy duty and running a Design Studio. A big shout out to her for all the time she has put into getting Feed produced.

Graphic design

Ruth Littlejohns-Sames
David Sames

Sames + Littlejohns
www.sameslittlejohns.co.uk

Photography and styling

Ruth Littlejohns-Sames
www.ruthlittlejohns.co.uk

Copywriting

Anna Kiernan
Amie Knights
Mike Scott

Copyediting

Anna Kiernan

Proofreading

Della Davis
Anne Littlejohns

Research and school pick ups

Jessie Higginson

Illustration workshop

John Kilburn
www.johndkilburn.com

The kitchen team

Georgie Travis, Shirley Thompson, Angie Douglas, Angus MacDonald, Ruth Clarke, Rosie Kingdon, Tomoko Currie, Sally Batchelor, Kay Patterson.

The dinnerhall team

Kath Vinnicombe, Nicola Brewer, Paula Mercer, Jenny Hackwell, Sarah Minter, Angie Snell.

The captain who navigates this great ship

Richard Gambier - Head Teacher

Marlborough School children

Gabriel Higgins, Gabriel Marshall, Madison Stanfield, Corbin House, Cordelia Iggulden, Deanna Merton, Faye Willow Williamson, Louie Mobley, Miriam Walsworth-Bell, Zeno Scott, Callum Webber, Chloe Baker, Eva Reid, Harry Dhiman, Jay Campbell, Joe Rhodes, Lauren Davis, Olivia Patterson, Bertie Blodau, Sasha Gowers, Scarlet Walker, Bailey Vinson, Eric Walsworth-Bell, Iona Statham, Leo Scott, Marcie Anthony-Moore, Marli Schoeman, Tudo Scott, Arella Espinosa-Payne, Ellie Currie, Ellie Prason, Esme Gowers, Felix Rodd, Fionn Glazzard, Fynn Seamark, George Bullen, James Power, Jenna Davis, Lilia Smith, Lucy Ellis, Luke Davis, Maddie Jose, Marley House, Matilda Littlejohns-Sames, Millie Stivey, Riley Harris, Roxanne Jenking, Sam Evans, Sebby Pryer, Beth Minter, Clara Scott, Dylan Hall, Jessica Crowther-Southworth, Lexi-Jade Reeve, Martha Kingdon, Oliver Swayne, Suki Semmens-Dobson, Tansy Grice, Theo Onciul, Toby Rowe, Tula Walker, Seth Littlejohns-Sames.

Print production

Just as we support locally sourced produce we also sourced a local printer!

Booths Print
www.boothsprint.co.uk

Print funding

LanesHealth
www.laneshealth.com

A humongous thank you to LanesHealth for funding the print and production of Feed. Their story began in 1930, when Gilbert Lane first created what is now a thriving and prosperous family company.

Initially working from his home in the Gloucestershire town of Newent, the business grew rapidly and by 1940 was operating from premises in the city of Gloucester. Gilbert was passionate about good health and the relationship between diet and well being.

He was an early supporter of the idea that we can improve our health through diet and the use of carefully selected plants and nutrients. As a result his company created a demand for special foods and herbal remedies intended to improve people's quality of life. In 1974 LanesHealth moved to brand-new, purpose-built premises.

Led by Gilbert's son Roger (who had qualified as a pharmacist) they developed their licensed herbal medicines which form the basis of their range today. It was also Roger who laid the foundations for bringing together traditional herbal knowledge with state-of-the-art manufacturing facilities. It is still this combination that ensures they are a leader in their field today.

And finally, you!

And finally thank you for purchasing Feed, enabling all the funds raised to go back into our school kitchen to be invested in children's workshops, equipment, field trips etc and who knows, maybe even another cookbook.

We did our best when putting the book together to test all of our recipes, but please keep in mind that each cook, each ingredient, and each oven is a little different. We hope they work for you like they do for us, if at first you don't succeed, adjust a little and try again!

ISBN 978-1-9998727-0-0
2nd Revised Edition
Copyright Marlborough School © 2017

Shall we eat outside?

You have a go

you wash I'll dry

I'll have the same as you.

TASTY

Shall we add more?

let's just USE our hands!

YOU try some?

what's next?